YOUR RIGHT TO KNOW
The Call to Action

**Presidential Right to Know Committee
of the American Library Association**

Edited by
Patricia Glass Schuman
Margo Crist
Elizabeth Curry

American Library Association
Chicago and London 1993

Project editor: Bruce Frausto

Cover and text designed by Donavan Vicha

Composed by ALA Production Services in Times Roman using
Ventura Publisher 3.0. Camera-ready pages output on a Varityper
VT600 laser printer

Printed on 50-pound Finch Opaque, a pH-neutral stock, and bound
in 10-point C1S cover stock by IPC, St. Joseph, Michigan

The paper used in this publication meets the minimum requirements
of the American National Standard for Information Sciences—
Permanence of Paper for Printed Library Materials,
ANSI Z39.48-1984. ∞

ISBN 0-8389-3428-5

Printed in the United States of America.
97 96 95 94 93   5 4 3 2 1

ALA Presidential Right to Know Committee

Patricia Glass Schuman, ALA President 1991–92

Margo Crist, Chair
Assistant Director for Public Services
University of Michigan Library
Ann Arbor, Michigan

Elizabeth Curry, Executive Director
Southeast Florida Library Information Network
Fort Lauderdale, Florida

Carol DiPrete, Director
Roger Williams College Library
Bristol, Rhode Island

Joan C. Durrance, Professor
University of Michigan
School of Information and Library Studies
Ann Arbor, Michigan

Elizabeth Futas, Director
Division of Library and Information Studies
University of Rhode Island
Kingston, Rhode Island

Margo Hart
Neal Schuman Publishers, Inc.
New York, New York

Nancy Kranich, Associate Dean
New York University Libraries
New York, New York

Patricia Mautino, Director
Instructional Support & Information Services
Oswego County Board of Cooperative
  Educational Services
Mexico, New York

Kathleen de la Peña McCook, Dean
School of Library and Information Science
Louisiana State University
Baton Rouge, Louisiana

Dorothy Puryear, Chief
Special Library Services
Nassau Public Library
Uniondale, New York

Joan Ress Reeves
Providence, Rhode Island

Merrilyn Ridgeway
Program Directional Specialist for the Wiche Program
Graduate Library School/Extended University
University of Arizona
Tucson, Arizona

Rhea Rubin, Consultant
Oakland, California

Subcommittee: Conference within a Conference
Buzzy Basch
Basch Associates
Chicago, Illinois

Joseph A. Boisse, University Librarian
University of California, Santa Barbara Library
Santa Barbara, California

Subcommittee: Library School Project
Sara Fine
School of Library and Information Science
University of Pittsburgh
Pittsburgh, Pennsylvania

Contents

Preface   vii
Patricia Glass Schuman

Acknowledgments   ix

SECTION ONE
   Your Right to Know: The Vision

A Diary of the Presidential Year: Goals, Efforts, and Impacts   3
Patricia Glass Schuman

The Rally and the Call for America's Libraries   7
RTK Committee and ALA Public Information Office

On to the Revolution
   Opening General Session Address   13
Gloria Steinem

Democracy and Libraries: A Vital Partnership
   Opening General Session Address   17
Representative Patricia Schroeder

Photo Section: "Lift Ev'ry Voice . . ."   21

SECTION TWO
   Your Right to Know: The Conference within a Conference

The Library Mission: To Secure the Right to Know   27
John N. Berry III

A New Way of Thinking about Librarians   34
Carla D. Hayden

Public Action Faces Public Policy: Supporting Our Right to Know   38
Cesar Chavez

Getting the Message Out   43
Susan Silk

The Call to Action   46
Charles E. Beard

Your Right to Know: The Profession's Response   51
Compiled by Joseph A. Boisse and Carla Stoffle

SECTION THREE
Models for Action: Marketing Your Right to Know
at State and Local Levels

How Librarians Help: Real Stories Found by Students
    in the Library School Project   57
Compiled by Joan C. Durrance

Speaking Up and Speaking Out: A United Voice in Washington
    and Idaho—A Project in Progress   61
Mary M. Carr and Barbara C. Greever

How Your Right to Know Took Root in Rochester,
    or Viburnum Are a-Bloomin' in New York State   65
Amy Small

Public Relations Campaign Plan   69
Texas Library Association

Bad Times Need Good Libraries   77
Massachusetts Library Association

Library Awareness Campaign   97
Maine Library Association

Preface

Patricia Glass Schuman, ALA President, 1991–92

When I took office as the 1990–91 vice-president/president-elect of the American Library Association, I thought long and hard before selecting a presidential theme. After consulting and brainstorming with groups of colleagues, I decided upon "Your Right to Know: Librarians Make it Happen." I chose this theme because libraries are one of America's most valuable and unique resources. Librarians are dedicated to ensuring the American people's right to know.

This theme was envisioned as being more than simply a catchy phrase—it was a prelude to mobilization and action on behalf of libraries, librarians, and the public's right to know. My presidential initiatives were based on the premise that we librarians work in a critical profession, fighting to serve this country's information needs at a time of fiscal crisis. We are opposing censorship, combatting restrictions on public access to government information, struggling to provide the resources and services that support a literate nation, working to provide free access to information services and technology, and attempting to preserve our heritage.

Your Right to Know: The Call to Action presents the essential elements of ALA's highly successful Right to Know mobilization. It covers the strategies used to implement this effort, the programs and speakers presented at the 1992 Annual Conference, the reactions of participants, and continuing initiatives to support and publicize the right to know.

"Section 1: Your Right to Know: The Vision" includes "A Diary of the Presidential Year: Goals, Efforts and Impacts" and "The Rally and the Call for America's Libraries." The first chapter describes both the experience of being ALA president and the Right to Know campaign; the second covers the two media campaigns ALA developed to call attention to the funding crisis in libraries and the importance of libraries and the right to know.

Gloria Steinem's "On to the Revolution" and Patricia Schroeder's "Democracy and Libraries: A Vital Partnership" complete the section.

The presence of Gloria Steinem and Patricia Schroeder reflects another important decision a president must make—who will be chosen to speak to the many thousands attending the opening general session. After much consultation and reflection, I selected two of the foremost women in America. This decision was based on my belief that equality and equity are two of the most important aspects of America's right to know. We all have the same right to information; the same right to knowledge; and the same right to the economic, intellectual, and personal benefits that information and knowledge can provide—whether we are black or white, rich or poor, young or old, male or female. But, tragically, there is a growing gap between the information "haves" and "have nots" in our society. And economics, race, culture, age, and gender often determine the dividing lines.

Gloria Steinem's chapter reflects her experience as a vocal and effective human rights activist who has encouraged millions of women to fight for our right to know about the issues that concern us: a right to know the facts that will empower us; a right to know that our other rights will not be violated; a right to know how we can be equal players in the democratic process; a right to know the information we need to lead healthy and productive lives; a right to know how we can make a difference. Pat Schroeder writes as one of America's most caring and respected political leaders. Her view is that without certain basic opportunities—to learn, to earn a living wage, to receive health care—a person's power to exercise his or her right to know is severely limited. Her paper shows her dedication to improving the quality of life for individuals and their families; her belief that education and libraries empower people and ensure their right to know.

"Section 2: Your Right to Know: The Conference within a Conference" contains the papers presented at the daylong President's Program that took place June 28, 1992. The format was inspired by the presidential programs of E. J. Josey and Clara Jones, on whose presidential commissions I served previously. Moderated by Margo Crist, chair of the Presidential Right to Know Committee, the Conference within a Conference was a day set aside for intensive discussion. Despite an incredibly busy conference, we took this time to explore together; to reflect on the right to know; to understand our roles as librarians; and to develop strategies to protect the right to know. We took this time to examine our profession in the larger context of our American democracy and the "information society," with all its problems, resources, traditions, myths, values, and various realities.

John Berry's "The Library Mission: To Secure the Right to Know" sets the philosophical context for the discussion. Carla Hayden's "A New Way of Thinking about Librarians" underscores the diversity, potential, and challenges of the library profession; Cesar Chavez offers an eloquent proof of the power of dedication and the right to know in "Public Action Faces Public Policy: Supporting our Right to Know." Susan Silk's "Getting the Message Out" offers professional advice for telling the library story to the media. Charles Beard's "The Call to Action" demonstrates the effectiveness of coalition building among all types of libraries and with other agencies. "Your Right to Know: The Profession's Response,"

compiled by Joseph Boisse and Carla Stoffle, represents an attempt to capture the flavor and spirit evidenced during the participants' small-group discussions.

"Section 3: Models for Action: Marketing Your Right to Know at State and Local Levels" focuses on concrete local or individual action. "How Librarians Help" results from a project of the Presidential Right to Know Committee and a number of library schools. Presented here are Joan Durrance's and Rhea Rubin's choices of the best stories gathered by library school students about how librarians help specific individuals exercise their right to know. "Speaking Up and Speaking Out" reports on the Washington and Idaho Library Associations' media training project, modeled on the ALA national Speakers' Network training that took place as part of the Right to Know campaign. "How Your Right to Know Took Root in Rochester" reports on plans for utilizing the major grant for public awareness that the New York Library Association received in September 1992. Reports on campaigns in Texas, Massachusetts, and Maine complete the volume.

Your Right to Know: The Call to Action is the second publication resulting from the yearlong 1992 Presidential Program and campaign. The companion volume, *Your Right to Know: Librarians Make it Happen: Conference within a Conference Background Papers,* includes my 1991 inaugural address and seven original papers commissioned specifically to provide background for the participants in the 1992 President's Program Conference within a Conference. Chapters were written by Leigh Estabrook and Sara Suelflow, Nancy C. Kranich, Kathleen de la Peña McCook, S. Michael Malinconico, Gary O. Rolstad, Mary K. Chelton, and Joan C. Durrance. Topics covered are political, legal, and ethical aspects of the right to know; access to government information; technology; literacy; youth; and the power of personal stories. This volume of background papers is provided at no extra charge with this new publication. Additional copies may be ordered separately from ALA under ALA order number 7621-2 for $6.00.

A major goal of the Right to Know campaign was to involve a broad spectrum of librarians. This volume represents something more than a simple recording of the history of this effort; instead it offers another avenue for readers to reflect, to learn, and to act. *Your Right to Know: The Call to Action* has been published to help the library profession and others understand exactly how librarians can make—and are making—the right to know happen.

Acknowledgments

The success of ALA's "Your Right to Know: Librarians Make it Happen" campaign, which provided much of the material for this publication, is a result of the dedication and involvement of many people too numerous to name individually. I am deeply indebted to the members of the Right to Know Committee and its subcommittees, (see p. iii) who worked long and hard to mobilize the profession and to launch and implement the program and campaign. Many thanks go to the authors included in this volume and the background paper publication. My special gratitude goes to Elizabeth Curry and her Editorial Subcommittee (Margo Hart, Elizabeth Futas, Mary Jo Godwin, and Kathleen de la Peña McCook) for developing and editing the background papers, copyediting the speeches, and planning this publication.

In addition, invaluable work was accomplished by Julie Todaro, who donated her time to train more than three hundred volunteer facilitators and recorders at Midwinter; Linda Wallace, who worked with us by telephone during many long nights to develop the message; Susan Silk, who taught us how to get that message across and made sure we were heard; Gerald Hodges and the Chapter Relations Committee, who helped organize the Speakers' Network; Charles Beard and Kimberly Taylor, who coordinated the Call for America's Libraries: Say Yes to Your Right to Know campaign; Eileen Cooke, Anne Heanue, and Carol Henderson, who helped with the detail and substance of the complex issues; and Bernie Margolis and Peggy Barber, who helped raise funds and other essential in-kind donations.

Among many, many others who provided inspiration and support are Jack Neal, Stan Epstein, Yolanda Cuesta, Gloria Leonard, E. J. Josey, Norman Horrocks, Kathleen Weibel, Pat Tarin, Carla Stoffle, Major Owens, Eric and Ilse Moon, Nancy Bolt, Pat Berger, and Richard Dougherty.

My warmest and deepest appreciation goes to Margo Crist, whose thorough planning and unswerving dedication and support were critical to all of my presidential efforts. And finally, my thanks to David Epstein and the ALA Publishing Department for their patience and faith in this book.

Finally, few of these activities could have taken place without donations from ALA's Library Champions and Advocates, whose names appear on the following page.

Library Champions ($5,000+)

Ameritech Information Systems

Baker & Taylor

Bantam Doubleday Dell Publishing Group Inc.

Brodart Co.

Cahners/R.R. Bowker

Data Research Associates, Inc.

Dawson Subscription Service, Inc.

Dun & Bradstreet

Dynix, Inc.

EBSCO Subscription Services

The Faxon Company

Gale Research, Inc.

Gaylord Information Systems

Grolier Educational Corporation

Grolier Inc.

The Highsmith Co.

The Library Corporation

McDonald's Family Restaurants

McFarland & Company, Inc. Publishers

Microsoft Corporation

Oryx Press

The Research Libraries Group, Inc.

Thomas Built Buses, Inc.

Simon & Schuster

Social Issues Resources Series, Inc.

Telephone Express

Times-Mirror

Waldenbooks

The H. W. Wilson Co.

World Book Educational Products

Advocates

Association of American Publishers

Demco, Inc.

the distributors

Dow Jones & Company

E.B.S., Inc. Book Service

Ingram Library Services, Inc.

Innovative Interfaces Inc.

Mountainside Publishing Co.

Neal Schuman Publishers

OCLC Online Computer Library Center, Inc.

Omnigraphics, Inc.

Otto Harassowitz
c/o Library Consultants

Pikes Peak Library District

Quality Books

Sirsi Corp.

Turner/A Faxon Company

UMI

Your Right to Know

The Vision

A Diary of the Presidential Year

Goals, Efforts, and Impacts

Patricia Glass Schuman

In the life of the American Library Association, 1992 was the 117th year—just one more year for ALA. But for me, as ALA president, it was the busiest, most thrilling (sometimes hair-raising), fascinating, exhilarating, and exhausting year of my life.

As ALA president I had an opportunity to see the American Library Association as others see it: a powerful voice committed to libraries. The power of the American Library Association surprised me. It awed me.

I have talked with, corresponded with, and met thousands of people—an elementary-school child planning a mock Newbery-Caldecott banquet, George and Barbara Bush. I have traveled to conferences from Moscow to Hawaii, and I've spoken nearly once a week to audiences of librarians, journalists, publishers, and, of course, the public.

Sometimes, we forget that ALA is a microcosm. Certainly, we have plenty of internal political problems and pressures, but we exist in the world; the macrocosm of war and peace, recession, budget battles, and a changing world order. We exist in a world that respects us, a world that considers us a powerful voice on behalf of libraries, librarians, and the right to know. During my presidency I tried to keep up with our internal action, while at the same time focusing our attention on the macrocosm.

Having watched and worked with many ALA presidents, I knew it was critical to hit the ground running. When elected in 1990 I had already decided that my focus would be the right to know. I chose this focus to celebrate the role we librarians play in ensuring this right and to call attention to what I believe is a national emergency: the fact that America's right to know is in serious jeopardy. People cannot exercise their right to know if their library is closed, if they don't know how to read, if they are not aware of the value of information or if they can't afford it, or if someone else is telling them what they should and should not be allowed to read.

We librarians are out there fighting to serve this country's information needs at a time of fiscal crisis. We are fighting the would-be censors; fighting to keep government information available; fighting to provide the summer reading programs, preschool story hours, and all the other resources and services that support a literate nation; fighting to preserve our heritage.

For many Americans, the library is their best hope of getting help. For some, it is their only hope. While libraries do not guarantee a literate and educated populace, they are mandatory for building one. Libraries and librarians have always been a part of the American dream: a dream that is dreamed in myriad colors and many languages. This dream is increasingly beyond reach for many people of color—and most particularly for their children.

To help focus ALA's attention on how libraries and librarians can contribute to making the right to know a reality for people of all cultures, I appointed a special President's Committee on Cultural Diversity chaired by Yolanda Cuesta of the California State Library and Gloria Leonard of the Seattle Public Library. Its two-year charge is to work with all units of ALA: to develop programs to recruit culturally diverse students to the profession, to

(WHCLIS); the second was the August IFLA conference in Moscow, which coincided with the failed coup.

Comparing the actions of WHCLIS delegates with the bravery of the Russian people may seem a far stretch, but the similarity in both cases was the determination of the people to uphold democratic ideals in the face of formidable barriers. The one-thousand-plus WHCLIS delegates assembled in Washington did not battle physical barriers like tanks and guns; they did fight and overcome all sorts of psychological obstacles: procedural foul-ups, technological bottlenecks, and both subtle and overt at-

---

Librarianship is the only profession *dedicated to the Right to Know.*

---

foster the participation and advancement of culturally diverse people within the association and the profession, to promote the delivery of library services to culturally diverse populations.

At Midwinter the committee sponsored an exchange of ideas and strategies with ALA affiliates and units, which resulted in a new publication entitled *Bringing Us Together: A Selected Resource Guide to Cultural Diversity.* Next year the committee will give minigrants to other ALA units to develop model diversity activities. Funding for a minority-recruitment videotape is being sought.

Crucial to the right to know are ALA's legislative concerns. Some weeks this year I spent more time in Washington than I did in my office. The ALA has an important and complex federal agenda. Funding cuts and information policies favoring privatization have been promulgated by both the Bush and Reagan administrations over the past decade. Their implementation, over ALA's protests, has made the Jeffersonian ideal of an informed citizenry a more distant possibility for many American citizens. With the help of the Legislation Committee and the Washington Office I have testified and sent numerous letters on behalf of ALA addressing issues such as privatization, funding for the Library of Congress, fees for government information, an electronic gateway to government documents, and changes to the standards for ethical conduct for federal employees.

During the summer of 1991 I witnessed two very different events, both of which demonstrate the true power people have if they are willing to fight for democracy. The first event was the July White House Conference on Libraries and Information Services

tempts to promulgate special agendas for private gain. The Russian people resisted those who attempted to abrogate their newfound right to democratic government; the WHCLIS delegates defended the American people's historic right to know.

The two events reminded me that the right to know—embodied in the First Amendment and in our system of library services freely available to the public—exists only in democratic countries. Totalitarian governments support schools, hospitals, armies. Only democracies support freely available library services for all residents, regardless of age, sex, status, or ability to pay. Certainly the intentions of the special interests who view information as a commodity to be bought and sold in the marketplace were more benign than those of the Soviet plotters. In both cases, the euphemisms were abundant. The Soviet coup leaders talked about "illness" (imprisonment) and "stability" (fascism); private interests battled with delegates to support fees for services and advanced proposals that talked about "adding value" (repackaging) and "diversity of sources" (privatization of government information services).

The defeat of proposals that would limit the public's right to know in order to fill the coffers of a few was a major victory for library users. Delegates consistently upheld the public's rights of free access to government information. The final WHCLIS recommendations were an affirmation of libraries, librarians, and library services.

My goal as ALA president was to propel the national school, public, and academic library story into the public eye, to make the public think about the importance of libraries and librarians, our uniqueness, and the crucial access to information we provide. Through the hard work, commitment, and dedication of many people we made progress, gaining widespread recognition and respect for libraries.

My proudest achievement is the Call for America's Libraries: Say Yes to Your Right to Know campaign. The highlight of my year was feeling the support for libraries and librarians from countless reporters, from all of our members who made the campaign work, and the hundreds of thousands of people who responded with concern and enthusiasm to say yes to their right to know.

When we planned the July 1991 Rally on Wheels, then-ALA-president Dick Dougherty and I took what some thought was too great a risk. But the ALA Rally on Wheels proved that ALA could move fast to address an issue of primary concern to its members: the growing crisis in library funding. Most important, it showed that when ALA speaks out, the American public listens. Because of that rally, the media's coverage of the library-funding crisis rose by more than 200 percent. Stories appeared in the Associated Press, the *New York Times*, *Parents Magazine*, NPR, CBS, the *Christian Science Monitor*, and local newspapers from coast to coast. Personally, I talked to numerous reporters, appeared on shows like "Larry King," CBS's "Nightwatch," and NPR's "Talk of the Nation."

For months following the rally I received several calls a day from reporters who were writing stories about local-funding crises and who wanted a national perspective. The most frequent question they asked was: "Why haven't you told us the library story before?"

The Rally on Wheels visited six cities. Only a small portion of ALA members and library supporters could participate personally. When the media called, the second most frequently asked question was: "When is the rally coming to our town?" So we figured out a way to bring the Rally for America's Libraries to many more towns across America.

With the help of the presidential Right to Know Committee, chaired by Margo Crist, and the ALA Public Information Office, we mobilized ALA's first Speakers' Network. Funded by an ALA World Book Award, media training was provided to ALA division leaders and state chapter representatives. Our goal? To mobilize librarians across the country to speak out through the media and in person on behalf of America's libraries and librarians.

The Right to Know Committee worked with ALA's Public Information Office and the Chapter Relations Committee to develop "power tools" like *The Right to Know: A United Voice*, ALA's first issues briefing book; a poster/tip sheet for the December issue of *American Libraries*; and a *Right to Know Campaign Book* to help us tell our story effectively.

The ALA Speakers' Network became the backbone of the Call for America's Libraries: Say Yes to Your Right to Know campaign. Charles Beard and Kimberly Taylor spearheaded the state-by-state effort. With help from Special Libraries Association (SLA) president Guy St. Clair, we enlisted the SLA Media Librarian's Division in our efforts to reach the media. Our objective was to speak out loudly and clearly, with a unified voice. And we did.

For the first time in history, we librarians went directly to the people of this country. We asked them to stand up and be counted for libraries and librarians. We may not have been competition for Ross Perot or Jerry Brown, but the 800 number sponsored by ALA and Friends of Libraries USA attracted more than seventy-five thousand callers and more than three hundred thousand signatures and letters from every state, the District of Columbia, Puerto Rico, the Virgin Islands, and Guam. More than a quarter of a million people told us they believed that libraries are essential to our democracy, that libraries are important educational institutions, that librarians are crucial to the information age, and that libraries of all kinds should be fully funded.

Retirees called and told us that libraries are the only way they can afford to read newspapers and magazines. Teachers pleaded for libraries to stay open for the sake of their students. Many people were angry, saying government officials should cut down on their own perks and put more money toward libraries.

When we began the Call for America's Libraries on Freedom of Information Day, March 16, we hoped for twenty-five thousand calls. We received three times that. With more money, more lines, and more time, I'm convinced we would have had ten times that number. According to telephone company estimates, only one in four callers could get through because our lines were so busy. When you consider that we did this in four weeks, on a shoestring budget, and with volunteer phone operators, those seventy-five thousand calls represent a tremendous outpouring of support.

The 800 telephone number was operative until April 11, when our funding ran out on the last day of National Library Week. The response had been so overwhelming we decided to continue the rally with a petition drive, hoping to increase our seventy-five thousand to one hundred thousand library supporters. We received more than three times that.

The Call for America's Libraries was a first, reaching out to millions of people because of extensive media coverage. Local spokespeople conducted more than two hundred radio and television interviews. Paul Duke of "Washington Week in Review" heard me on a Washington public radio show and decided to devote an entire segment to the campaign. "CBS This Morning," CNBC-TV, and Monitor TV news also aired substantial stories. I was interviewed by almost every major radio network.

Print coverage included editorials and news stories in newspapers across the country, as well as a *Christian Science Monitor* editorial, an editorial note in the *New York Times*, and a column in *USA Today*. The *Washington Post* carried a cartoon that showed George Bush saying, "Read my 'lops': no more libraries!"

Most important, the American people spoke out. They gave us their support, their time, their signatures, their testimony to the significance of libraries and the right to know in their lives. Across America—from Anchorage, Alaska, to Bangor, Maine, to Honolulu, Hawaii—

leadership in the fight against budget cuts. The ALA Washington Office reports significantly higher awareness of library-funding issues among congressional staff.

But what delights me most of all is that ALA members have decided to be silent no more. The Washington and Idaho Library Associations jointly applied for and won this year's World Book–ALA Goal Award. They are using the grant to undertake a regional speaker-training project—patterned after the National Right to Know Speakers' Network; and the New York Library Association has received a $335,000 grant from the Viburnum

---

More children participate in summer reading programs (estimate 700,000-plus) than play Little League baseball.

---

newspapers carried stories on librarians, libraries, and the right to know. All told, there were an estimated five hundred stories about or inspired by the Call for America's Libraries.

The incredible show of support gave us tremendous leverage when we walked into the Capitol to present our results to Congress on June 17. We met with House Minority Whip Newt Gingrich, Senate Majority Leader George Mitchell, House Majority Leader Richard Gephardt. They were impressed by our numbers and appreciative of the documentation that would help them in overriding the president's proposed budget cut for libraries.

Many more good things have come out of the high visibility achieved as a result of this remarkable campaign. Twelve new corporate "Library Champions" signed on to support the campaign, bringing the total to more than $100,000 from thirty-six corporations. New York Mayor David Dinkins pledged to restore five-day-a-week library service. New York and Brooklyn Public Library officials credit ALA with providing national

Foundation to plan a major campaign on behalf of libraries. This summer the New England Library Association offered media training for the state association officers from that region.

It has been an honor and a challenge to serve as president of the American Library Association during a year in which, to paraphrase Charles Dickens, we have seen some of the best and worst of times for our nation's libraries. This has been the longest and the shortest year of my life. I have never felt so stimulated or so proud. This year I've truly seen—and helped to use—the power and prestige of this association to help preserve America's right to know.

Serving as president of the American Library Association has been extraordinary and spectacular because of what ALA represents to librarians and to people who love and respect libraries: people who value their right to know. Together we spoke out; we spoke loudly, and we spoke proudly. I am confident that we will continue to make a critical difference for Americans and America's libraries.

The Rally and the Call for America's Libraries

RTK Committee and ALA Public Information Office

"Librarians Vow to Get Word Out"
Atlanta Constitution, June 30, 1991

"As Libraries Face Cuts, Supporters Plan a Protest"
New York Times, July 8, 1991

"Let's Hear It for the Libraries"
Christian Science Monitor, July 9, 1991

Those were among the headlines as the American Library Association launched a historic campaign—the "Rally for America's Libraries"—at its 110th Annual Conference in Atlanta.

The goal: to mobilize public support for libraries, librarians, and the most basic of America's freedoms—the right to know—at a time of devastating funding cuts for school, public, and college libraries. The rallying cry: "Libraries are worth it!"

"Without question, this rally is an historic event," declared Richard M. Dougherty, 1990–91 ALA president, at the kick-off rally attended by some 4,000 librarians and friends of libraries.

"It's the first time librarians have taken to the road. It's the first time we've ever said we won't be quiet anymore, because we have a story to tell."

"This is not the end; it's the beginning," added Patricia Glass Schuman, 1991–92 ALA president. Colorful banners and signs carried the messages "Kids who read succeed," "Save money. Fund libraries" and "Libraries are worth it!"

On July 4, Dougherty and other ALA leaders boarded a bus to take a Rally on Wheels to six southeastern cities and a final rally in Washington, D.C., before the opening of the White House Conference on Library and Information Services.

The unprecedented campaign focused local, state, and national media attention on the plight of libraries, with coverage by, among others, "CBS Sunday Morning" with Charles Kuralt, the Larry King Radio Show, National Public Radio, *USA Today,* The *New York Times,* and the Associated Press.

Phase two of the campaign, the Call for America's Libraries, was launched under Schuman's leadership on Freedom of Information Day, March 16, 1992. It featured a special toll-free telephone number and a petition drive for the public to "Say Yes to Your Right to Know."

A grand total of 311,374 people from every state (also Guam and the Virgin Islands) registered their support by picking up the phone or pen during the unprecedented campaign. The total included letters and petitions signed by 253,631 people and 75,743 who called the toll-free number. The call-in campaign ended at midnight, April 11, when funding for the toll-free number ran out.

Millions more were made aware of the crisis in library funding as a result of extensive media coverage that included televised reports on "Washington Week in

Call for America's Libraries

Highlights

- ALA President Patricia Schuman and campaign cochair Charles Beard present the campaign results on June 17 to key Congressional leaders, including House Minority Whip Newt R. Gingrich, (R.-Ga.), Senate Majority Leader George J. Mitchell (D-Maine), and House Majority Leader Rep. Richard A. Gephardt (D-Mo.).

- Total number of calls and letters: 311,374

- Total number of media placements: approximately 500

- The ALA Washington Office reports significantly higher awareness of library funding issues among Congressional staffs as a result of the letters from constituents and media coverage generated by the campaign.

- Media interest in libraries continues at a high level. "CBS This Morning" carries a report on libraries as part of its Moneywise segment (April 12). *Northwest Airlines* magazine carries an article on ALA in its April issue. The *Congressional Quarterly* (June 22) focuses on "Hard Times in Libraries."

- Twelve new corporate "Library Champions" sign on, including McDonald's and Waldenbooks.

- New York Mayor David Dinkins pledges to restore five-day-a-week library service at the city's branch libraries in May. Officials at Brooklyn and New York public libraries credit ALA's leadership.

- Charles McDowell gives an impassioned report on the crisis in library funding on the PBS news commentary program "Washington Week in Review" (April 10).

- The *New York Times* (April 10) endorses the campaign, stating, "In this election year, there'll be no better vote."

- *USA Today* columnist Barbara Reynolds praises the contributions of libraries and librarians, urging, "If you think librarians are worth fighting for, you have until Sunday to call 1-800-530-8888 and fight back" (April 10).

- Every major radio network and news service, including AP, UPI, ABC, and the Independent Broadcasters Network, carries interviews with ALA President Schuman.

- The Cable Business News Network and The Christian Science Monitor Channel carry televised reports on the library funding crisis. The *Christian Science Monitor* newspaper publishes an editorial, "Dialing for Library Dollars."

- The New York Library Association receives a foundation planning grant for major funding of a high-profile public awareness program patterned after ALA's efforts.

Rally for America's Libraries

Media Highlights 1991–92

National Public Radio, "All Things Considered," June 5, 1991

The *Atlanta Journal Constitution,* June 30, 1991

"MacNeil/Lehrer Newshour," July 1, 1991

Mutual Broadcasting System, July 4, 1991

"CBS Sunday Morning" with Charles Kuralt, July 7, 1991

New York Times News Service, July 8, 1991

USA Today, July 8, 1991

The Christian Science Monitor, July 9, 1991

Knight-Ridder News Service, July 10, 1991

Larry King Radio Show, July 15, 1991

Associated Press, July 24, 1991

Parenting magazine, November 1991

"USA Radio News," Independent Broadcasters Network, March 14, 1992

Media Culture Review, January 1992

WBZ-AM, Boston, March 16, 1992

KFWB-AM, Los Angeles, March 16, 1992

ABC Information News, March 16, 1992

NBC News, March 16, 1992

KQED-FM, "Forum," March 17, 1992

Governing magazine, March 1992

WMAQ-TV, "Chicago Live," April 6, 1992

Cable Business News Network, April 7, 1992

WGN -TV, Chicago, April 9

WNBC and the NBC-TV network, April 9, 1992

WRC-TV, Washington, D.C., April 9, 1992

New York Times, April 10, 1992

"Washington Week in Review," April 10, 1992

USA Today, Barbara Reynolds' column, April 10, 1992

The *Christian Science Monitor,* editorial

The Monitor Channel, April 10, 1992

The Washington Post, April 20, 1992, "Washingtoon"

Utne Reader, May/June 1992

Reading Today, April/May 1992

Congressional Quarterly, June 22, 1992

Penthouse, July 1992

USA Today Magazine, July 1992

Review," "CBS This Morning" and the Cable Business News Network; and editorials in the *New York Times, Christian Science Monitor,* and *USA Today.*

Altogether there were an estimated five hundred media placements in radio, television, and newspapers from coast to coast, including many "radio rallies" with ALA President Schuman, members of the ALA Speakers' Network, and local librarians discussing the crisis in library funding and rallying public support.

Those who called and signed petitions were asked if they agreed with the following statement:

"I believe America's libraries are essential to democracy; I believe libraries play an important role in education and that librarians provide vital services. I believe our nation's libraries should be fully funded."

On June 17, an ALA delegation headed by Schuman and campaign cochair Charles Beard of West Georgia College presented the campaign results to key Congressional leaders, including House Minority Whip Newt R. Gingrich, (R.-Ga.), Senate Majority Leader George J. Mitchell (D-Maine), House Majority Leader Rep. Richard A. Gephardt (D-Mo.), Sen. Mark O. Hatfield (R-Ore.), and Rep. Major Owens, (D-N.Y.), the only librarian to serve in Congress.

The Rally for America's Libraries was financed almost entirely with contributions from corporate friends of ALA and libraries, including those listed in the front of the book (see page x).

Call for America's Libraries

Comments

There's a big problem with illiteracy here. They say there are 17,000 people who read at less than third-grade level. They're going to take away funding that's potentially an answer. I wish you the best—not just for you—but for me and my kids.—Beryl Amedee, Houma, Louisiana

I am a working-class father with four children. If it weren't for libraries my children wouldn't be able to succeed as well as they do in school because of the services that America's libraries afford working-class people who can't afford computers and the widget and gadgets. I just want you folks to know that I believe the funding they want to take away from you is barbaric. I thank you for listening.—Ted Shattle, Iowa

I'd rather give up my food stamps than the library.—Unemployed man

Continued on page 11

"Say 'Yes' to Your Right to Know" Campaign
March 16–June 16, 1992

State	Calls	Petitions	Total
Alabama	547	16,803	17,350
Alaska	504	535	1,039
Arizona	2,173	2,763	4,936
Arkansas	406	378	784
California	7,386	15,633	23,019
Colorado	2,213	10,202	12,415
Connecticut	1,150	3,212	4,362
Delaware	661	1,455	2,116
Florida	3,615	2,077	5,692
Georgia	1,745	13,539	15,284
Hawaii	384	89	473
Idaho	246	1,590	1,836
Illinois	3,980	3,564	7,544
Indiana	795	138	933
Iowa	1,039	274	1,313
Kansas	1,177	18	1,195
Kentucky	636	552	1,188
Louisiana	2,200	6,237	8,437
Maine	576	17,000	17,576
Maryland	1,586	5,739	7,325
Massachussetts	2,905	5,579	8,484
Michigan	1,819	1,816	3,635
Minnesota	2,811	2,214	5,025
Mississippi	544	7	551
Missouri	803	9,918	10,721
Montana	579	1,654	2,233
Nebraska	533	2,581	3,114
Nevada	446	834	1,280
New Hampshire	567	152	719
New Jersey	1,541	4,638	6,179
New Mexico	478	220	698
New York	10,727	8,313	19,040
North Carolina	3,199	263	3,462
North Dakota	87	53	140
Ohio	5,714	51,195	56,909
Oklahoma	547	1,974	2,521
Oregon	1,724	492	2,216
Pennsylvania	1,747	2,424	4,171

State	Calls	Petitions	Total
Rhode Island	800	995	1,795
South Carolina	663	2,838	3,501
South Dakota	609	200	809
Tennessee	1,723	5,603	7,326
Texas	2,792	1,369	4,161
Utah	239	135	374
Vermont	632	1,967	2,599
Virginia	1,327	2,822	4,149
Washington	615	120	735
West Virginia	310	5,760	6,070
Wisconsin	1,219	3,217	4,436
Wyoming	2,134	3,758	5,892
Dist. of Columbia	260	3,167	3,427
Guam	1	0	1
Puerto Rico	4	0	4
Virgin Islands	0	180	180
Grand Total			**311,374**

Yes, libraries are essential to democracy, definitely deserve more funds, play an influential role in education (boy, do they!) and are certainly vital players in the information age . . . Our right to know is a freedom we don't want to live without. Libraries are "where it's at."—Marty Norton, Kingman, Arizona

I can't imagine my life without libraries . . . They're essential.—Erika Opper, San Francisco

What would our country do without libraries? Let's invest more in our public library systems so that they can become even better!—Ida Fern Charles, Scottsdale, Arizona

They just announced they're going to shut down our bookmobile. My children and I depend on that bookmobile. The school library was closed about a year ago. The nearest public library is twenty miles away. What are we supposed to do?—Mother of two, upstate New York

I consider a cut to libraries as much a threat to my intellectual health as a cut in public health services would be to my physical health.—Seventy-five-year-old man, retired on limited income

Our nation is suffering an educational crisis. Now is the time to support free access to information through our libraries.—Carolyn Fisher, Director, ISMMC, Inc., New York

Books, not bombs! Knowledge is our best line of defense.—C. J. Riedel, Victor, Iowa

I went every week to storyhour as a child. That's something I want to share with my kids . . . If they go cutting funds, there may not be a storyhour. They're using a volunteer now . . . I want this to be a tradition for my children.—Debbie Baswell, Cookeville, Tennessee

There's no greater thing than libraries. I couldn't live without them. I go there all the time and I'm never disappointed.—Wayne Ramond, Raleigh, North Carolina

We hope that the impact of this brilliant campaign extends throughout the United States, helping libraries, librarians, and especially the democratization of knowledge in the three Americas.—Katia M. Lemos Montalli, Campus University, Trinidade, St. Catarina, Brazil

We've had a lot of comments about public officials. I've

had some who say cut the Congressmen's salaries and fund libraries, that Congress should give up their banking and free health services and put the money toward libraries.—Susan Smith, operator, phone bank, Colorado Springs, Colorado

It's pitiful—not like when I was a kid. You can't check out biographies, myths, and fables. They're considered reference materials. The books on the shelves are ragged and colored on.—Freelance writer, Brooklyn, New York

I've been going to the library since I was three year old. I still go there and sit in the children's section. I think that's where children really grow up in ways that they would never have a chance to. Everything is open to them there. Reading made me what I am.—John Pappas, Silver Springs, Maryland

I don't know where I'd be without a library open full time.—Barbara Lorselle, Milton, New Hampshire

I just want to say it's very important to support libraries and that libraries should not be cut. Many people depend on libraries. Many children learn to read from library books.—Woman

It would be a shallow and deprived community, indeed, which did not enjoy the services of a public library. We must assure that our public libraries do not fall by the wayside for lack of funding or other resources to support this most worthwhile endeavor. Our best wishes for your success.—Gil and Mary Kay Gordon, La Grande, Oregon

Public libraries provide so many opportunities for people of all ages, both educational and entertainment, and they must receive the federal support needed to continue to operate.—William Jack, Rochester, Indiana

Please count on us for support of libraries, librarians, and most importantly, our right to know.—Brenda and Bill Lee, Wileyville, West Virginia

I just want to say I support the library. I support any

legislation and I don't want libraries cut back. Libraries are very important.—Gene Sanders, Jefferson, Ohio

I want to say everything good I can. The Hart County Library is the best thing there is. I'm eighty-two years old and I can call down there and get anything I want. My grandaughter told me to call you. We're book people.—Madora S. Walker, Hartwell, Georgia

They'll waste money on all sort of things. They don't seem to care about the newer generation. My wife borrows about a thousand books a year. I wasn't a very good student but my kids are doing great and they use the library all the time.—Fifty-year-old man, Trinity, North Carolina

I buy books and I use the library. I am very supportive. I don't want to see them (libraries) go by the wayside.—James Cornish, Fredericksburg, Virginia

Our mayor is trying to save money. He has proposed to close the three local branch libraries. I feel a local library is very important. We use the library a lot. You get a great deal of help from our small library. I feel it's vital to have a library close. A lot of people can't drive to a library, especially older people and school children. I just want to do something. It should be your right to have a library around.—Marjorie Moon, Warwick, Rhode Island

I just want to register my concern. I just found out that my library has had to cut back one of my favorite magazines (*Poetry*). It's sort of expensive. Librarians are very helpful.—Mary Rose Dougherty, East Montpelier, Vermont

I've been heartsick at our local situation and that it means curtailment of hours at our library. We recently lost our librarian. She went on to a better position. I want to express my gratitude that there is another library nearby in another community even though it's facing financial difficulty too. I collect books and I'm so grateful that the library is there for research and information. I hope there won't be more curtailment of funds. They're critical, especially with our economy the way it is now.—Barbara Wasko, Bridgeport, Connecticut

On to the Revolution

Opening General Session Address
at ALA Conference, June 1992

Gloria Steinem

Thank you for inviting me to be part of this very important and historic meeting and for putting me on the platform with so many good hearts and minds. If only the White House looked like this platform we would have a very different [world]. Of course, I confess that every time I hear that I'm one of the twenty-five most influential women in the country, I realize in what deep shit we really are.

I've come here to say thank you and to invoke you to even further revolution [in regard to] your very important and very influential Right to Know campaign. Indeed, I think that even revolution is probably an inadequate word for what women have to do and for what women and men who are protectors of the endangered library system have to do. What has been meant by *revolution* is just taking over the army and the radio stations, right? That's very small potatoes. We have much more in mind than that. We have to transform relations between women and men, between races, between classes. We have to get rid of the old hierarchical systems based on race, sex, and class. We have to transform old ideas of a European-centered or Western-centered world. We have to transform ideas of who should have the information and secrets in society and who should not. And libraries are the forefront, the front lines of this revolution.

But first I'd like to say the thank-you part. The thank-you part is very personal because I was one of those millions of people whose childhood was rescued by libraries. In Toledo—anybody here from east Toledo? the libraries of east Toledo? Well, due to the vicissitudes of my family's wandering around the country in a house trailer, I didn't go to school for a full year until I was in the sixth grade. I'm probably entirely a product of libraries. You've made me what I am today, and I hope you're satisfied.

I used to go especially, I remember, to the tiny branch library in east Toledo, and I used to read. I just thought it would be boring to read this way [pointing horizontally, across imaginary shelves]. I was starting out to read all the books in the library. So I read this way down all of the stacks. I read Nancy Drew and the Hardy Boys. In some way, having no direction is quite helpful; I didn't know that the Hardy Boys weren't written for me. I read *The White Oaks of Jalna* and *Forever Amber*. Remember *Forever Amber*? Only the golden oldies here know how daring that was. I read Louisa May Alcott's *Little Women* and *Gone with the Wind* simultaneously and over and over every year from the age of about six to twelve. That will show you how schizophrenic I really was.

But I do wish to thank you from the bottom of my heart and not just for myself but for all the people whose lives were transformed, literally transformed, by access to a library. Of course later, because of *Ms.* magazine, I also came to owe you all a debt of gratitude for your fight against censorship. There were always many cases around the country in which the ultra-right wing was trying to take *Ms.* magazine off the library shelf. It seemed that we were a kind of early warning system for censorship, in fact, because if they could keep you all from paying for a subscription, which was easier to do, since that was an affirmative action, then they had established the precedent and could remove other books from the shelf. Anybody here from the Mount Diablo school district? This happened mostly in school libraries, and it was there that one of the premier cases was fought, and because of the resistance of school librarians it came to the public's attention, and in the end it served to change the character of the school board as people won elections

his voucher system. I begin to [see the politics] of information. That whether it is weather information or census facts that we are being asked to pay for, or to give money to private organizations for, information that has been generated by tax dollars belongs to all of us.

As a feminist I thank you for your efforts to include [rather than exclude our material in libraries]. I'm sure that you have noticed how easy it is to tell the difference between right-wing agitation and feminist agitation. One is asking you to remove things from the library; the other is asking you to include more things in the library. It's

---

Every writer knows that all books begin in the library, and if you're lucky—they end there.

Richard Peck, author, crew member of the
Rally on Wheels and Library Hero

---

on this issue. I also want to thank the eight thousand folks in libraries who have supported the new ad-free *Ms.* magazine. Thank you so much. But I feel I owe an apology to some of you who supported *Ms.* during its Australian incarnation, when we did not control it and thus you did not get your subscriptions completely fulfilled. It went into something resembling bankruptcy and interrupted its publication. So I'm happy to say that there is a *Ms.* magazine booth here [at the ALA conference exhibits] and I hope you will come meet us there. If we owe you, if we have not fulfilled your subscription, I hope you will tell us, and I will endeavor to go out there and raise contributions to get you your subscriptions and not to contribute to the deficit already being suffered by libraries.

As a writer, of course, I know how many people there are who come up to me in bookstores and say that they can't afford my book or someone else's book. Of course, I frequently tell them to steal it, but I also direct them to libraries as you also do. And because I come from New York, where even our great library between the two lions on Fifth Avenue is suffering great deficits, I understand what it's like to have to raise money constantly, with endless benefits and social events, in order to keep going what should, of course, be a public trust and one that our tax dollars [should] support. As a citizen I'm becoming more aware of how important libraries are, of how much they are our last democratic, educational institution. I see the efforts, the sinister efforts, to undercut our public school system on the part of everybody from Benno Schmidt, former president of Yale, to President Bush and

very simple, and I appreciate from the bottom of my heart your efforts to include multicultural material to make clear that we are addressing all people. And I can only say that as I see the results of self-esteem studies showing that women's self-esteem diminishes with every year of higher education, and that children in general, but especially boys and girls of color, find their self-esteem diminished by education, I begin to understand how important it is that we have books, many, many diverse books, in which people can be seen in their real positions in the world and can perceive themselves as central. Sometimes I think that we should have an effort called the Nannerl Mozart Memorial Fund. Nannerl [Marie Anna] Mozart was Wolfgang Amadeus Mozart's sister. We didn't see her anywhere in [the film or play] *Amadeus*, but in fact they traveled through Europe together playing the piano as child geniuses. Many of his compositions may have been hers. We only know about her because of the letters that were written by Amadeus to her after she went home to be married off at sixteen and become a teacher of other musicians. We know that he considered her, however, the really talented one. And there are so many examples throughout history of female people, of people of color, of people of the "wrong" sexuality, who are never even identified [because of judgments about them or] their true life-style [and so they may have] changed history [but are hidden from us so they should not] be seen as admirable.

I thank you for all of your efforts in all of these struggles. It seems to me that there is no group more on the front lines of every struggle, whether it is government funding, education, censorship, the inclusion through multiculturalism, and through a feminist opening of the other eye, than librarians, and I thank you for that. But I must say that all of these areas of thanks are also reasons why I would like to urge you to a new radicalism, a new activism, and a new stage of revolution. We have to be very careful that we don't fall victim to what Patricia Schuman, your ALA president, has called "the impotence of virtue." We must see ourselves as the revolutionaries we truly are.

because I didn't know where the proper picket line was. [Answering a shout from the audience] Minneapolis, all right, I'll be there. I'll either come and march with you or stay away, whichever is most useful.

But I wonder if we do not need a new radicalism to follow the very important information campaigns that you have mounted and the very important efforts to pressure the political system. It seems to me that we are on the verge of a danger to libraries so drastic, [which I have seen] as I travel around this country, that it is a parallel almost to the burning of libraries and [the loss of]

We marched for the right to vote, we marched for the right to equal access, we marched for the right to open housing, and now we'll march for the right to read.

Rev. Jesse Jackson, shadow senator,
District of Columbia

You are the most important and democratic source of information. Ironically, since fully half of our gross national product is devoted to the production and the distribution of information (without even counting all the things that are not in the gross national product at all, like childbearing, homemaking, and all the unpaid, uncounted, invisible labor that probably would drive this up to at least seventy-five percent of the gross national product), and still [we] are not properly valued and, I think, that often we are not properly valuing ourselves. If you are the place where society goes to find itself, you are the last refuge of those who don't have terminals and modems and so [are] on their own. I've come to wonder if we are not turning into a society that could be best described as one containing people with information and without information, if it is not a far more sinister plot, whether conscious or not, that we are becoming a country of the information rich and the information poor.

And, finally, since you are also a disproportionately female profession with all the attendant problems and understanding of powerlessness, you understand the problems of other powerless groups. But you also have the attendant power of numbers, of numbers of change agents in this profession. I notice that although I've marched on many picket lines in my life, I've never marched on a picket line with librarians. I've marched with nurses. I've marched with secretaries. I've marched with secretaries of the Nine-to-Five organization and from the pink-collar ghettos, but never with librarians. Now perhaps this is just

history that we so mourn, [if it is like] the burning of the great centers of learning in so many instances in the ancient world. Is that not what is happening when we pay per capita for each student about a third of what it costs to purchase one book, and when we consider the per capita amount contributed to libraries for all the people who use them, [and] it is so small that I have not even been able to discover its measurement? We need to use the methods of all the great social justice movements. We need to march; we need to demonstrate; we need, perhaps, a tax strike. Remember during the days of Vietnam, some of you here probably participated in the tax revolt, which meant that we deducted from our taxes the amount of money that went to Vietnam and then essentially said to the government, okay, come and get it if you like. We notify you that we are keeping this aside. Well, what would happen, I wonder, if enough of us took the amount of money that we, or the ALA professionally, calculates belongs to libraries, [and] gave it [directly] to the libraries and said to the government, "We have allocated our tax dollars; now come and get it."

We need to learn from the AIDS groups, for instance, that are teaching us all what activism is. We need to use some of those kinds of methods to save our libraries, and, in general, we need to feel our own importance as librarians and the kind of esteem and honor that allows us to act radically, consistently, unapologetically with humor, with enthusiasm, with intransigence, on our own behalf.

Usually when I end a talk like this, a brief talk, I have in the past declared all of us to be something like part of the international revolutionary feminist government in exile, and I think that we are, of course. Feminism simply means opening the other eye. It's as if we have been looking at the world with one eye closed, but if we open the other eye and see the world as if women mattered, then we see a very different reality. It doesn't change everything completely, but it transforms everything substantially. We also begin to take away the paradigm of subject-object, of inferior-superior, on which racism and class and all of the other inequalities are built. Inequality between two people is the beginning of hierarchy. Hierarchy is based on patriarchy. Patriarchy doesn't work anywhere anymore—at home, in the office, anywhere. It is the model of subject-object and also the justification of aggression. Olof Palme, the great, now deceased chief of state of Sweden, said it was the foremost responsibility of all the governments in this world to humanize, to uproot the gender-based political system, because that was, he said, the greatest cause of violence in the world, and we can no longer afford that kind of violence on this fragile spaceship Earth, which we love so much.

But I've come to notice that when we say words like "revolution," "exile," and "government," we sometimes key into old ideas in our heads. Those are words we have heard before, and they sometimes narrow our dreams rather than set them free.

So I will instead try this out on you. I haven't quite come to a substitute but try this: Suppose we are here today for this convention, and when we return [home we] begin to see ourselves as the Secret Society of the Butterfly's Wing. Even the most conservative physicist will now admit that the flap of a butterfly's wing here can change the weather thousands of miles away. Everything we do matters, and the art of acting morally is behaving as if everything we do matters. One child who comes in and gets one book because of your efforts; one library that is kept with doors open for one more hour; one politician whose mind is changed; one civic structure that can no longer afford to shortchange libraries because they understand this is the hot political issue, this is the one that is really going to get them in trouble, get them demonstrated against, get them picketed outside their own homes, in fact, not just their offices; one act of this kind on each of our parts can truly make a difference that will change the weather thousands of miles away for many people.

So my heart goes with you at this convention. I realize that the stereotype of librarians is not that you are on the front lines, but the stereotype of women all together was not that we were on the front lines. I confer honorary womanhood on all of the men here, and I look forward to marching on picket lines with you and to a revolution begun in libraries that will have no end, and that will change the world's weather.

Democracy and Libraries

A Vital Partnership

Opening General Session Address at ALA Conference, June 1992

Representative Patricia Schroeder

I am delighted to be here with the cultural elite. I couldn't follow a better speaker than Gloria Steinem inciting you to revolution in the kinder, gentler way. Gloria is absolutely one of our national treasures. I would have never been elected if she had not come to Colorado twenty years ago to see this young thing who was running for Congress out in Marlboro country. When I walked out and said, "Hi, I'm thirty-two years old and I think I'll run for Congress," there were people falling on the cement and laughing. But Gloria had the courage to come out and stand up for me. I will never, never be able to thank her enough.

This is a very difficult time, yet a very important time, that we are looking at, and so your convention could not be more timely. I think that is why so many of you probably hocked the family jewels to get here, but what a terrific turnout. To me that says you really are ready to start flapping your butterfly wings and changing the climate in Washington.

There are a lot of reasons why this administration has been cutting back on libraries. First of all, how can you be an education president and have a budget that cuts back funding for libraries seventy-six percent? That's amazing. Most politicians know an uneducated constituent is their best consumer. You can tell them anything, and if you tell it to them long enough, they will believe it, especially if you do not have any libraries where they can go to look up your voting record. Most newspapers have stopped printing voting records. It is getting harder and harder to find out how a politician voted. Libraries seem to be one of those great repositories and they are a real threat to the people in Washington and business as usual. Obviously, we have to do everything we can in to make sure that they have trouble.

That is part of it, but there is another part, too. There really is something going on in this society that is creating a two-class society. It terrifies me. There are many in Washington who don't understand the library issue at all. If you want an education, if you want a library, you are supposed to be a member of the lucky sperm club and inherit one. Actually I am being sexist. I guess you could be a member of the lucky egg club, too, and inherit it. When you look at our history, a lot of our forefathers and foremothers would be horrified. Think about Jefferson. Thomas Jefferson wrote the inscription for his own tombstone because he did not want anybody messing it up. He did not put on it that he was an ambassador and a president. He did not think that was important. He inscribed on it things about freedom of speech, freedom of religion, his part in attempting to establish those as fundamental principles of this great government, and that he left all his money to found the University of Virginia because he felt the only way democracy could work is if everybody had access to public education and could go as long and as far as they could possibly go. It did not depend upon who your parents were.

One of the big differences was that many people came to this country because in other countries you were what your parents were, but in this country you were what your children could become. How can they become what we want them to become if they don't have access to information? I am appalled that the state of California, which used to lead this great country, is now at the very rear. If children in California want to go to a library, they are much more apt to be able to if they are in a correctional institution. That is sick. That is very sick. Think about what that means. Think about how far we have *not* come. Evolution is not working in politics. It is not working at

billion means. That is a lot of money. That is way more than my state budget. Believe me, we could divide my state budget into that and go on for almost ten years. My real question is, who are we spying on? How are we going to have anybody that can even do intelligence in a couple years if we are draining off things like libraries to fund it? What kind of craziness is that?

Think about the budget debate we had at the beginning of the year. The administration had insisted that we build walls in our budget. There had to be a wall between domestic spending and military spending and another wall between foreign aid and domestic spending. The

---

As a young person growing up in Hot Springs, Arkansas, I have many fond memories of the time I spent in the Garland County library. . . . As a student . . . my love of learning was fostered and enhanced by all the resources I made use of in the libraries where I studied. . . . Today as a father, I encourage my daughter to use and enjoy all the treasures that can be found in the library.

President Bill Clinton

---

all in politics. When you think that we were a country of just a few million people turning out Jeffersons, Madisons, and Washingtons and we all stand up and cite them. Now here we are, a great country of 250 give-or-take-a-million people, and we are producing Quayles and Helmses and Strom Thurmonds and so forth. There are many that you would like to make honorary redwoods and move on.

Benjamin Franklin had this radical idea that libraries should be free and that they should be public. When you look at that incredible heritage, and you see how far we have moved from it in a time when we are the richest country on the planet, you have to wonder what has happened. Think about how silly we must look to other countries. Here we are one of the wealthiest countries on the planet and we have people standing around saying we can't do anything, there isn't any money. Well, we could do a lot of things. The issue is our priorities. Think about our priorities. The president's budget cut libraries 76 percent, but it funded Radio Free Europe. Isn't Europe free yet? There is over (I can't tell you how much because I would be in trouble—this is a classified secret) thirty-five billion dollars being spent on intelligence—thirty-five thousand million dollars. That is what thirty-five

administration lived in mortal terror that someone like me might transfer a few dollars over and buy some books for some libraries, or get some shots for some kids, or up the Head Start funding, or do something really crazy like that. So they needed these walls and behind these walls you could not transfer one dollar over the top. At the beginning of this year some of my colleagues and I tried to take those walls down. We figured that if the Berlin Wall and the Iron Curtain had come down and the Soviet Union had imploded, maybe we could take the walls down in the U.S. budget. The answer was, no, the walls stayed. Every one of you ought to find out how your elected officials voted on that and ask them why. Why are we spending more on defense this year than the whole rest of the free world added together spends? What are we doing with this huge intelligence budget? What are we doing with all this other stuff that is out there and cutting libraries seventy-six percent? That absolutely is not the wave of the future.

Part of what happened was that in the 1980s we really lost our way and government became more and more about control. It scares me. I think we are into some deep fundamentals this time. There is the fundamental of how the federal government treats more than half of its population, women. Are we are or we not going to be treated as adults? There is going to be a very interesting discussion about that during this election. But there is going to be another fundamental. Are we going to allow all Americans maximum access to the information and knowledge that they are going to need so desperately in this global universe we live in? Is there anyone who believes we are going to make it by knowing less in the next decade? Does anyone believe that we can do it with less education, less knowledge, and less information? If they do, I wish they would come to the stage. I would love to debate

I am for the America that was for democracy. I am for the America that believes democracy will work only if people are educated. To be educated they must have access to information. That bring us right back to Ben Franklin, who insisted we have libraries that are free and public, open to all so that all citizens can participate. That is the America I believe in. I am for the America that believes that if you want to change the world, you change the world of a child. That is the America I believe in.

I am frightened when today half of America's public libraries no longer have librarians for children. That is

We in Washington need to hear these messages so we won't forget how important libraries are to the education of young and old.

U.S. Rep. Liz Patterson (D-S.C.)

them. We have a government that has been spending our money trying to control the rest of the globe. You know we **are** the United States of America. We're number one. Dial 911. We will go anywhere at anytime to protect anyone no matter how rich or undemocratic they are.

I never mind doing our part, but I think our part has become the whole part in so many instances. We had an interesting time in Washington recently when Boris Yeltsin came to town. I could not help but sit there and think, what a difference a year makes. One year ago the polls showed President Bush with a ninety percent approval rating. A year ago Gorbachev was considered the most popular world leader on the planet. If I had stood in front of you a year ago and said that one year from now Saddam Hussein will be in office and Gorbachev will be history, you would never have believed it, and yet here we are. What a radical change. How are we going to process this? It is going to be very difficult. Think about the fact that in one day the average American reading the *New York Times* is exposed to more information than the average person living in seventeenth-century England was during his or her whole life. We are being subjected to all sorts of change, but we need our roots. We need to stay in touch with our history, with our foundation, and with the institutions we have built. That way we can really have some structure and really think of where it is we are going. Are we out to protect emirs of Kuwait because they have oil even though they do not believe women should vote or drive a car? We sit by in a "ho hum" fashion and watch all sorts of horrendous things going on in Yugoslavia, but they don't have any oil. What is our value system?

tragic. If we do not care about our children, we do not care about our future. I am frightened because in the 1960s we made a covenant to our children. I did not say promise to children, I said covenant. Adults can deal with political promises. They know that is politics. They all know this, but children don't. Children believe it. Adults tell them they are going to do this and they believe they are going to do it.

In the 1960s, we said the federal government would have all children ready to learn when they were delivered to the schoolhouse door at age six and that we would fund immunizations, feeding programs, and Head Start. The government also made another covenant. It said that if the children did well in public school, then when they were ready to go on we would fully fund the Higher Education Act so that all children could go as long and as far as their abilities would take them. That was the 1960s. Now it is the 1990s. Half the children in Washington, D.C., have not had their shots. Only a third of the eligible children in America are in Head Start. We are not even doing a feeding program in Los Angeles for babies past their eighteen-month birthday. When they reach eighteen months old, they are off the feeding program. I was in Los Angeles two weeks ago talking to young people in the riot zone. They were saying we will take used books, we will take anything. That is what they want. They want to read, they want out, they want hope, they want up. Thank you, Debbie Allen, for realizing that and pointing that out. Can't we hear them?

I work in Washington, D.C., where to deal with education we have had one more great study, Education

2000. The number one thing it says is that by the year 2000 we hope to deliver six year olds to the public schools ready to learn. That is forty years late. Have you seen waste in any of these programs? Nobody has found a waste in libraries. No one has found children lining up for the second round of shots because the federal government is giving them out. Nobody has seen any of that.

So we ought to get mad and we ought to be speaking up because the country that doesn't care about its kids doesn't care about its future. I am very scared. If you look at the 1980s, everything in the federal budget went up except money for children—it went down. We now have more kids in poverty, more kids needing your services than ever before. But school boards and government officials everywhere are cutting back on those services. Those children will never have that opportunity. They can not hang out and wait twenty years for the economy to grow again so the library can reopen. They can not climb into a freezer and freeze themselves and then defrost suddenly when we have money again to accommodate them. We cannot afford to lose this generation. This is not spending; this is investment. This is our heritage and our forefathers would be furious that we have been so lax and let it slide so far.

There is another thing going on, and librarians should be talking about this. There is another notion in Washington that we are going to automate everything. We don't need librarians. Well, first of all, I cannot even work a toaster, so the more automated it gets the more I need a librarian. It is like in the early days of the Automat when it was said that we will never again need waiters. Well, we found out we really do need waiters. We need human contact. The Automat is gone. We need librarians more than ever because of the information overload, the complexity, and all of the audiovisual resources. If you don't have someone showing you how to use them, then you lose them. So librarians are more important than ever before. It is absolutely essential that we do not let politicians think that they are just going to have some little automated thing on the corner and that we do not need any more libraries.

We need to get you fired up. This is one of the most critical years this country has ever had. It is an election year. We are starting to see wonderful things happen. In California everybody is singing the Beach Boys song about California girls, but they don't mean surfers. They mean Diane, Barbara, and all of the wonderful women running for the congressional seats. If the Beach Boys had written songs like that in Pennsylvania and Illinois, we would be singing those songs, too, because we really see this whole synergy of new people ready to move into

Washington. The wonderful thing about it is that as all of the voting profiles show, for every woman voting for them there is also a man. These men and women are saying we are going to reclaim this government and set new priorities. So it is not men versus women. It is men and women coming together saying we like these candidates' priorities—their priorities on young people, education, reading, learning, investment, and getting something back, and that is very good.

We have now engaged in a terrific debate after the unrest in Los Angeles. The federal government wants to rush in and spend all this money on weed and seed. They basically want to spend it all on weeding. That means they are going to go through and find the bad guys and lock them up. They have been doing that now for twelve years and we have more people in penitentiaries than any other country has. We also have more crime than any other country has. My message, and I hope your message, is to forget weed and seed. Let us try the old one of feed and read. Feed and read will get us much farther.

I cannot call you to the barricades any more eloquently than Gloria Steinem just did. I can only say that the public's image is that of "Marian, the librarian." We are all passive and we will not get out there and fight. Information is the best tool that we have. You are not Marian, the librarian. You are the lions outside the New York Public Library and you are ready to take them on. Let's do it! Let's get the candidates' voting records out there. Let's remind people that the way folks voted when they were in office is a much better predictor of how they will vote in the future than how they promise they will in the last month before voters go to the polls. Third graders know this. I do not know what has happened to the adults in America that they allow everyone to redefine themselves in an election year. Do not let them redefine themselves. You have their voting records in your libraries. Dig them out. Tie them around their necks. Do what we used to do—have a thousand sheets printed up that would say, so-and-so voted against libraries. You would send him a copy of that sheet. Write, "Dear Senator so-and-so, I have a thousand of these in my purse. I am taping them up in restrooms wherever I go. I am sticking them in menus. I am handing them out to my friends." This is the kind of thing we have to do. Because when America knows, America will change its voting pattern. This is a wake-up call. This is the time to say the 1980s are over. They were an aberration. We are back to our tradition. We are back to where this great country belongs. We are going to feed and read. We are going to have another generation of which we are very proud.

LIFT EV'RY VOICE...

*Images of the Rally and the Right to Know Campaign
from Atlanta to D.C. to San Francisco*

Above: All aboard the rally bus in Atlanta. From left:
ALA Executive Board members Betty Blackman and
Ann Symons, 1991-92 ALA President Patricia Glass
Schuman, 1990-91 President Richard Dougherty,
and crew members Joseph Boisse and John Hilinski.

Right: Thousands of library enthusiasts
supported the kick-off rally in Atlanta.

Above: Richard Dougherty
speaks out during the "Rally
on Wheels" at Greenville
County Library, S.C.

Below: Young readers join
U.S. Rep. Newt Gingrich
(R-Ga.) to support the
library cause.

Above: Garfield leads the Rally cheer in Greensboro, S.C.,
enthusiastically assisted by 1992-93 ALA President Marilyn
Miller.

Above: Library leaders carry the Rally message to Washington, D.C. Ralliers marching with 1990-91 ALA President Richard Dougherty include Ann Symons, Joe Boisse, Margo Crist, and others.

This [Washington, D.C.] is a place where they say education is the number one priority. Our job is to show it's hypocritical, stupid, and ridiculous to talk about the importance of quality education when they're closing libraries.

U.S. Rep. Major Owens

Above: 1991-92 ALA President Patricia Glass Schuman (center) and 1993-94 President-elect Hardy Franklin (left) review the Rally petition with U.S. Rep. Richard Gephardt, D-Mo.

Library Power at the Capitol: Holding the list of 300,000 supporters of the Call for America's Libraries are (from left) Jean Ann McCartney, director, Missouri Library Association; Nan Blaine Hilyard, director, Auburn (Maine) Public Library; Patricia Glass Schuman, 1991-92 ALA President; Charles Beard, campaign co-chair; and Hardy Franklin, 1993-94 ALA President-elect.

Above: Author Gwen Davis, head of Writers Who Love Libraries, discusses shared concerns with guest speakers Gloria Steinem and Rep. Pat Schroeder in San Francisco.

Above: Rep. Pat Schroeder (D-Colo.) addresses the Opening General Session of the ALA 1992 Conference.

Right: Patricia Glass Schuman,1991-92 ALA President, addresses the Opening General Session of the 1992 Conference.

Above: Cesar Chavez, leader of the United Farm Workers, at the Conference within a Conference, flanked by Patricia Glass Schuman and U.S. Rep. Major Owens, D-N.Y.

Right: This bookmobile from Thomas Built Buses is a symbol of the generous support given by many Library Champions that made the Rally and the Call campaign work.

Your Right to Know

The Conference within a Conference

The Library Mission

To Secure the Right to Know

John N. Berry III

I wish I had been there when the American revolutionary Thomas Jefferson found "life, liberty, and property" among the human rights John Locke had asserted. Jefferson became my hero because he committed the greatest editorial act of U.S. history when he changed the word "property" to the phrase "the pursuit of happiness" before he put the words into our Declaration of Independence.

In that seminal moment Jefferson predicted the issue that has dominated our national debate ever since. At our birth as a nation, those revolutionaries asserted our inalienable rights in the central document of their—our— American Revolution.

Then, in a second stroke of genius, Jefferson spelled out the job of government. Here's how they put it in the Declaration of Independence: "To secure these rights, governments are instituted among men." That was our succinct revolutionary theory:

> All people are created equal. They possess, at birth, certain self-evident, inalienable rights. The task of human government is to secure and protect those rights, the rights of the governed.

Our inalienable rights exist independent of property or any economic or political system. We have them whether we exist under capitalism, socialism, a free market, or a regulated one. We'll return to that later.

The scientist/novelist/philosopher C. P. Snow conceived of an intellectual world divided into two cultures: an intellectual dichotomy with science on one side and the arts and humanities on the other. Adherents of either side were unable and/or unwilling to understand the other or to cooperate with each other. That rift between those two cultures obscured other early warnings of the time, the fifties, even though Snow himself pointed to economic dangers ahead. (C. P. Snow, *The Two Cultures and the Scientific Revolution* [New York: Cambridge Univ. Pr., 1959])

Those other warnings, warnings to which we have now begun to attend, suggest not only the emergence a third culture, but possibly global dominance by it. Today, in all of the West, in the liberated if embattled Eastern bloc, along the Pacific Rim, even deep in Asia, people have come under the dominance of that third culture.

Now the nations of what we have called the Third World are becoming engaged in a new mercantile imperialism. In short, all of the world has been taken over by that third culture.

That third culture is the culture of commerce, the culture of the free marketplace. Today, in its moment of greatest power, it overwhelms any and all things that stand in its way.

The free market has always been a dominant idea in

our country, despite the many ways it is regulated, aided, and abetted by government and entwined in the workings of government. Our American Revolution was rooted in mercantile issues, with questions of tariffs and customs duties atop our agenda as we tossed the tea into the Boston harbor.

At its most extreme, as in the United States, Germany, and Japan, the third culture has taken on the characteristics of a new religion or a new ideology. Nations now "mobilize" to win market share in a highly competitive world. Citizens are coerced to save money in order to facilitate capital formation to drive the acquisitive engines of an ever-expanding commerce. They are encouraged to borrow and spend to fuel the consumption of products, consumption to pay the price that will add to profits.

Whole regions of the world, like Western Europe or the Arab states, now form market alliances, new cartels to gain advantage—market share—in this brave new world culture. In Japan and Germany, government and industry are as indistinguishable as they once were in the Communist East or the Fascist past, but market share is the new target, market dominance the imperial goal.

Now our allies are princes or emirs, sheiks or ayatollahs, despots or drug lords, as long as they are willing to do business, to go to market with us.

Now governments exist to protect market share and, if ours is any example, to bail out corporations and businesses when they take bad risks, become entangled in foreign competitions, legal systems, or despotisms, and cannot buy their way out, like oil corporations in the Persian Gulf, freewheeling savings and loan bankers trying to make a fast buck, or defense manufacturers trying to exploit cheap labor south of the border.

Our country is one of the most militant marketplace societies, and it is probably the leader in converting the world to the third culture. At the same time, because we think we invented the game, we think everyone else is playing it by our rules. Thus we are surely the most naively idealistic about the idea. Americans see some kind of value-free, entrepreneurial capitalism as the perfect system. The Japanese and Germans, our earliest pupils of the market game, the third culture, were there centuries ago. In modern times, drawing on their traditional alliances between their governments and businesses, they have truly changed the way the game is played. Our country has yet to learn how to enlist government in its profit drive, largely because here, unlike in Japan and Germany, government is viewed at worst as the enemy of the marketplace and at best as an annoying obstacle to free commerce in all things. In the United States, alas, to point out that every want and need cannot be forced into those ubiquitous market mechanisms, to suggest that industries must be regulated for safety and health or to preserve our environment, or to advocate that market manipulations of currency and people be curbed, that the great orgy of buying and selling land, companies, and, of course, products and services be constrained by rules aimed at fairness and a higher living standard for all people—even to suggest that we pursue these once-common social goals—is now to commit heresy, if not treason.

As the twentieth century ends, this third culture has so inundated the other two cultures, so captured them (using its standard weapons, money and power) that both science and the humanities are now enlisted in and committed to the major work of the third culture: the accumulation of individual and corporate wealth and power.

We now read best-sellers, not great books. We program what was once called educational television using the same measures as commercial television—ratings. We crush labor unions, even those of our air-traffic controllers, because they stand in the way of a totally free, totally uncontrolled market in air travel. We support global free trade, regardless of its impact on workers in Michigan or Louisiana, on our industries, or on the ownership of our land. And we even allow thieves like Milken and Keating to keep a few million from their ill-gotten gains.

In our country we privatize aspects of government that were tax supported and government operated from the beginning: roads, government information, parts of transportation. And now, God save us, they want to inflict market-type competition on our schools and education. We already know how that works in library education: You close private library schools, even though public universities not only get big enrollment from them, but also make money on them. Now they want to contract out libraries to private firms that have never been very good at library service.

Among these new marketeers it is considered a fact that information is a marketplace commodity, despite the obvious fact that it has none of the properties of a commodity.

To oversimplify that point, when you buy, sell, trade, share, give away, or even steal information (as those insider stock brokers, lawyers, and bankers did when the marketeers' recent boom peaked), when you do all that with information, you still have it. It is not scarce like all other commodities, and it is never consumed. When you use it, you still have it.

Despite our naive love for the marketplace, and our innocent hope that we can achieve what our business-people like to call "an even playing field," the rest of us in America know more about the dangers in the modern drive for world adoption of this third culture, the effort to create a world society dominated by markets rather than governments.

It is to our shame that we are not telling the world the whole story of a market society and the corruption, cheating, and dysfunction it can bring and has brought to so many aspects of our lives. We are not telling about the unemployment brought by free trade, the poverty and discrimination encouraged by weak government, the decline and collapse of great public systems in education and libraries brought about by a selfish, self-interested market-driven society.

The third culture, you see, takes as its enemies government and the public sector. The slogan under which it operates is still popular in America. It has always

lies in our ability or our lack of ability to make a case for free libraries and free access to information. Our potential for failure constitutes the greatest current threat to free information and thus to democracy, for we must have the former if we are to maintain the latter.

Right now, as a profession, some of us at least seem to be very much in tune with these times and the current American attitudes toward government. Some of us seem primed to go along, perched on the edge of a fundamental change in attitude, a change in our ideology if you like.

The best bargain, of course, is at the country's fifteen thousand libraries—where the books are free.

Barbara Bush

been. It goes like this: Government must not intervene unless the marketplace fails.

Our debate, as a result, has always been over what constitutes marketplace failure and thus requires government intervention.

At this moment, the advocates—or should I say "purveyors"?—of the third culture, the marketeers, are busily claiming victory in that set of debates and in the battles that have resulted. The ravages left by their victories, however, and the questions left unanswered by their rhetoric provide ample room for restraints on their worst excesses, if not reversal of the direction of events, and ample room for a strong, convincing rebuttal of their most specious assertions, like that one about information as a scarce commodity, some kind of depletable resource.

The impact of their success in our world of information and libraries has been massive. The results have been disastrous to the support of libraries in our country.

The questions remaining for librarianship probe down to the very roots of our calling. I label it a "calling," for there is no other way to explain why we love this library work, even though we alternately hate the conditions under which and the compensation for which we do it. We break our backs for compensation that puts us among those paid the least for the time and money we spend on education or for the commitment to service that we require of ourselves.

The current message emanating from Washington and Wall Street, from Tokyo and Berlin, is: No, the public sector should not exist, not even to the extent that it traditionally has.

The greatest promise or the greatest threat to the future of libraries and the citizens' right to information

Some of us are apparently ready to abandon our public mandate, our mission, our traditional library faith. Some of us are ready to trash the fundamental philosophy, that set of principles that has undergirded the development of one of the greatest systems of public libraries in the world.

To support or even be passive in the face of this change is to become part of the worldwide assault on traditional community values. It is to echo that almost universal and total disenchantment with government, and to rush to laissez-faire individualism in every area of activity, in every corner of the globe. As I said before, we have exported only part of the message to our former allies and enemies, neglecting to tell them the whole story about the disarray and corruption in both our industry and our government at all levels, about the stench of stealing and inequity that has enveloped America.

Decades ago, back in the sixties, we Americans still believed in government. Indeed, we believed that not only could we govern ourselves, but that through government we could bring new levels of equity to our society. Our political and ideological moods are different now. We've developed a new meanness. We are more than disenchanted with government solutions on every front. In the United States, our traditional suspicion of government, our basic American distrust of government, and our revolutionary antigovernment roots have hardened into a solipsistic fever, a raging individualism. At its best, it says that our guiding principle ought simply to be: To each according to his or her ability regardless of the rules, of human needs and human suffering, regardless of a body politic increasingly uneducated and ill informed.

Into this environment enter the predictions of futurists and many of our library colleagues. They offer a brave new world where print is replaced by the VDU. It is, of course, a marketplace, a paperless marketplace in which the machines transform all of our information needs into profitable packages of information. These electronic packages are sent and received at something called a workstation, one of those ubiquitous VDUs in that future that shows up not only in our office, if we still have one, but in our home, and probably in our bedroom, since we won't want all that plastic junk messing up the living room, dining room, or kitchen.

Libraries as we know them are obsolete in that paperless, ultrafree, dog-eat-dog market society, that completely deregulated information society in their predictions. Libraries, we know, have never been the main or sole source of information, although they have always been a unique source. Libraries are not now nor will they ever be even the main source of expertise on searching and finding vitally needed information from machines. (They actually do more of that than anyone else.)

You can probably guess by now that I do not believe this fiction, this library science fiction, this technofantasy being preached by so many men and women from platforms in industry, academe, and even libraries.

Neither do I believe the social science fiction of some of the current so-called leadership in librarianship, that small cabal of U.S. public librarians who have apparently bought the fads and fashions and Reaganomics of the free marketeers. That group sees the so-called discipline of marketing as the panacea for libraries. If only we can show the world how much we can sell library service to an unsuspecting public, they say (mostly through bookshop-type displays and collections with thousands of copies of the current best-selling trash), we will prove how effective we are.

As the new marketeers have predicted the privatization of much of government, these fashionable librarians of the Reagan-Bush era like to say that the user fee is a normal alternative source of revenue. They constantly remind us that what they call "realism" demands that libraries consider fees. They say, as an erstwhile ALA leader once said, "It is not a matter of whether or not libraries charge fees, but how much."

They have bought the rhetoric of business, so, of course, they like to see themselves as "competitors" in some information and entertainment marketplace.

From that idea they move on to suggest that if it is a marketplace the library is in, its services and collections should simply reflect what the public demands, like any enterprise in that marketplace. That demand, of course, is shown most often through recorded circulation of what the public uses. Librarians in that marketplace need not make any qualitative judgments about a book or a video-

cassette or an audiotape. All they need to do is look at its advertising budget and its TV tie-ins to predict public demand and then simply collect the materials needed to meet that demand.

They eschew any leadership role for the intellect, for any conception of literary quality, and they turn away from any responsibility for guiding, for inducing citizens to read and seek full information, to find excellence in literature or video. They prefer, instead, to operate as free or fee-based stores, purveying the same junk as the rest of the media and the shopping malls. Indeed, they truly love shopping-mall public libraries and hate big central libraries, academic libraries, and, with a special venom, any library that pretends to serve a research clientele.

Their libraries become too-little, too-late reflections of the worst of the yuppie materialism and rampant, mindless individualism that has lately infected U.S. society and now threatens to spoil other parts of the world. Their libraries become free Walden bookstores just when even Walden is beginning to realize that those highly selective, totally market-driven little bookstores just don't have enough stock.

Their libraries become places to shop, not places to listen, to learn, to venture into new fields. Of course, I reject this view of librarians as storekeepers.

Listen! There is another side to our profession and our country. There is a deeper belief in the book, in education, in full information, and in the responsibility of government to secure and protect the individual's right of access to that treasure. There is a bedrock American belief, dating from our Declaration of Independence, that governments are instituted among humans to secure the right to know.

Yes, most of us still reject those storekeeper library futures. And while we reject this kind of thinking, and therefore reject the notion that the best management model for libraries comes from commerce, from that third dominating culture, it is not just simple sentiment that sends us into that position.

Assess how well that model has worked where it has been the dominant method for a long time, in corporate North America. It is the free, unregulated market that brought us environment-killing variety in kinds of automobiles and in the amount of scarce energy they burn and the amount of garbage they emit into the air. It was the Madison Avenue–created demand for convenience and speedy solutions to life's minor problems—like the messy paintbrush, the sticky eggs in the frying pan, the unruly hairdo—that brought Teflon and the aerosol can, not to mention a host of wonderfully wasteful plastic and polystyrene packages.

Despite success in providing that kind of individualized waste in that overkill of variety, marketing and management methods did not show Canadian Campeau how to run a chain of stores; or show those Texas wheeler-dealers, including George Bush's son, how to run a savings and loan institution or a bank; or show Mr. Lee Iacocca how to compete with cheaper Korean and Japanese labor or how to actually earn his obscenely high salary; or show NBC how to hold on to Rockefeller Center in New York, now bought and owned by Mitsubishi.

The entire world watches in horror as we try to recover from the crises created by the free markets in oil and weapons, without which there would have been no Kuwait to tempt the Iraqis, nor an Iraqi military power to attack. There would be no tin-pot despot like Saddam Hussein for us to vanquish in order to protect the billionaire playboy sheiks, who own and milk Kuwait so they can buy more women to bed.

While my own company was owned by Xerox, we watched that huge conglomerate be more successful at building bureaucracy than our government was, more successful at buying financial houses to diversify its corporate lusts, only to see them fail in that bureaucratic environment. To top it off, as soon as the Xerox patent protection (provided by government) expired, that great, bumbling corporation forgot how to do what made it great, produce copying machines that could somehow compete with those of the Japanese.

Not all the modern management, all the marketing expertise, all the financial genius in the world, could save Xerox from that cheap labor, that alliance of government and industry, that national drive to win in the world that has brought us the flood—or should I say "glut"?—of Japanese products we now face.

That business model didn't save Lockheed or the savings and loan industry. It didn't stop the thieves on Wall Street from issuing tons of worthless junk bonds. It didn't save the great department stores.

To the extent that any of these has been saved, it has been by government intervention and taxpayer bailouts. That freewheeling, freebooting market mentality didn't even work in the very marketplace from whence it came.

So ask Michael Milken, ask Lee Iacocca, ask Canadian Campeau, who has bankrupted Bloomingdale's. Ask Macy's. Ask Captain Maxwell.

And when you mix these models, as some of those yuppie librarians want to do, you get even worse results. Look how well your post office or mine works on a combination of subsidy and fees. It doesn't work. Look at what we used to call educational TV in the United States. At the beginning of the television era we agreed to set aside a channel of our public airways for education. It was never the most popular programming, but it did its educational job pretty well, with stuff like "Sesame Street," "Nova," and some effective documentary work.

But the managers of educational TV discovered that free-market model. So we created a "corporation" for public broadcasting, and it measured effectiveness in that good, old-fashioned, marketing way: the rating systems. So the programming began to include talk shows and stuff like horror-movie series and a lot of imported British soap operas and bad comedies and films and Dick Cavett and a host of things that made it look suspiciously like NBC, CBS, and ABC.

The government, now ready to privatize everything, said, "Hey, we don't need another network at taxpayer expense." So it cut the public-broadcasting budget. Public TV turned to private fund-raising, and for corporate donors it would display the company's logo. As its need for funds increased and it wanted more, it let those companies give a little message. Guess what? Now public television is almost exactly like commercial television. But despite all that great marketing, management, and all, it is still nearly bankrupt. Thus it is forced to devote even more time than ever to fund-raising and to those noncommercial messages from corporate donors.

If the U.S. polls, library-budget votes, and bond issues we watch are any indication, recent expressions of public sentiment on public policy indicate that the pendulum has begun to swing back from its most extreme position against government intervention. Even so, in the United States, dealing with an immense federal deficit will probably mean much more damage to America's public institutions and government. There is clear evidence that voters are ready to use taxes and credit to support public programs when it is clear that the public at whom they are aimed believes in the programs.

Even the businesspeople with whom I ride airplanes are ready for a little more government, if it is a more enlightened government. And God knows, whether it is in air travel, the financial markets, commuter traffic, or, alas, international trade, they grudgingly agree that we need a little reregulation. In fact, they may agree that we need some other form of taxation to correct the awful inequities visited upon our local governments, which are totally dependent upon property taxation.

Public support for libraries during these antigovernment reactionary times never really diminished, thank God. That reservoir of political strength, which we librarians have so reluctantly tapped, is still intact in most jurisdictions in North America. We librarians are finally beginning to recognize that it is there, to understand the nature of it, and to join the public in an effort to rebuild the public libraries that were so badly hurt by the decades of austerity that hurt all public agencies in the United States.

As for information, we are beginning to convince them that it actually has the characteristics of a "free good" in economic terms. It is also a quintessential public good in historic and economic senses and in the more current, social, political, and practical senses as well. Let me read my favorite passage from economics:

> Lighthouses. These save lives and cargos, but lighthouse keepers cannot reach out to collect fees from ships; nor would it serve an efficient social purpose for them to exact an economic penalty on ships who use their services. The light can be most efficiently provided free of charge, for it costs no more to warn 100 ships than to warn a single ship of the nearby rocks. We have here a positive externality, a divergence between private and social advantage. Philosophers and political leaders have always recognized the necessary role of government as provider of such goods.

So say American economists Paul Samuelson and William Nordhaus, calling the lighthouse "a typical example of a public good provided by government service."

Information, like the light from a lighthouse, is a free good, and access to that information is a public good, worthy of government subsidy and tax support.

That's the crucial difference. Libraries are institutions created to meet needs, not wants, not demands. They were created to serve the educational, informational, and some of the recreational needs of people. While that mission sometimes overlaps with the marketplace, and indeed libraries do disburse products like books, magazines, and videocassettes from and into that marketplace, they are not truly part of it. They are publicly supported, libraries are, because our society decided that libraries are a public good, institutions worthy of public support. Libraries were created like the rest of our government with the mission to secure and nurture our rights—in this case, our right to know.

I said libraries are unique. They are similar to but, basically, fundamentally different from the other sources of information in crucial ways. Yes, libraries are still a crucial source of information. They could even be considered one of the media in terms of providing access to information for millions. It was American publisher Dan Lacy who first elaborated on the difference between access to information as found in a library and that found through other sources or media, in a speech he gave decades ago at a library school seminar. I've never forgotten the message. My paraphrase of Lacy's idea goes like this: Libraries are one of the information media. The other media, broadcast media, are forced to select from the immense information produced in modern times that small portion that will fit into a half-hour newscast, a daily paper.

The information vendors aim their packages of information at carefully segmented markets, chosen because they can afford the price, need the very narrow and specific data, and thus return a profit to the vendor. In this enterprise, they don't care as much about the number of people who buy access as they do about the return on their investment, the dollars they collect in making access available.

The library, on the other hand, collects all the knowledge of humankind, in all the formats. It collects all the information, unedited, unscreened, unrewritten, and, instead of broadcasting it to the masses, organizes and focuses that information on the individual. To that it adds a warehouse full of quality recreation, reading, and viewing that provide the kind of inducements to be informed that have been part of the public library mission since its beginning. All of this focuses on the individual and individual inquiry.

Despite the richness of information that libraries provide to nearly sixty-five percent of the population on a regular basis, in their entire history public libraries in the United States have never received more than two percent of the costs of municipal government. Usually they get a great deal less than two percent. When you add the costs of state and local government together, library expenditures are point thirty-nine percent of the total costs. That's right—nationally, libraries get less than four-tenths of one percent of the money spent on state and local government.

So here's at least one source of information, one way to gain access to it, that certainly qualifies as a public good in terms of the cost for each additional use. It may not be as efficient as a lighthouse, but it comes damn close. There are many other sources, closer to the original information itself, that are easily and cheaply shared among millions. The library secures our right to know efficiently and cheaply.

This point was strongly made by the trustees of the Boston public library as long ago as 1852, when they realized that they needed a public library, a public good to help inform the citizens of Boston. The private, fee-based libraries that existed in Boston in 1852 didn't do the job because, like all private-sector sources of information, those information packages and products didn't pay any heed to a general need for access to information. They were "adventures and speculations for private profit." Then they came to the point:

> [I]t has been rightly judged that—under political, social and religious institutions like ours—it is of paramount importance that the means of general information should be so diffused that the largest possible number of persons should be induced to read and understand questions going down to the very foundations of social order, which are constantly presenting themselves, and which we, as a people, are constantly required to decide, and do decide, either ignorantly or wisely . . .

That is talking about a government agency's responsibility to secure a basic, inalienable right, the right to know. The library of the future must return to that exalted mission. Even though the information and entertainment media it uses, and the technology available for the information function, will surely make it seem different, the mission is really unchanged: to secure the right to know.

We have learned some lessons in this mixed up twentieth century, but we have many more to learn.

We didn't end war or international hostility. But after World War II, Korea, and Vietnam, only an idiot would not readily concede that it is not an effective tool for international relations, for bringing change. We have proved that again in the Arabian deserts and in the Eastern bloc.

We also learned that whether you are Richard Nixon, Kurt Waldheim, Pierre Trudeau, Henry Kissinger, Caspar Weinberger, the ayatollah, or the prime minister, it is tough to keep secrets.

We learned that the Soviet Union was neither an evil empire nor a utopia. We are learning that the same, alas, is true of the United States.

We are learning that free trade is not everyone's cup of tea, and that is probably because it means different things in Tokyo or New Orleans or Mexico City or New York or London. It means different things if you farm or work in a factory or buy and sell on the international market.

We learned that, yes, you can make money selling and marketing some packages of information, delivering some messages. I do that for a living. We are learning again, however, that if your mandate is to meet needs instead of to slake market-driven desires, if your mandate is to get the message to everyone whether or not he or she can afford to pay the toll, if your mandate is to provide full information for all the people on a one-on-one basis, then you probably cannot make money doing that.

If your job is to secure the right to know for an entire society, revenue and profit are not the measures of success.

We are learning again that that is a job for government, and that government is managed for the people, and the bottom line, the measure of its success, even in this era of the third culture, is different.

The measure of government's success, of library success, is how well informed the people are. Are they so well informed that they can find meaningful, sustaining work? Do they know enough to be happy or, as Jefferson said, to participate in "the pursuit of happiness"? Are they well enough informed, most important of all, to govern themselves in a hostile and complex world?

I believe that the answer to each of those questions is yes! But the answer really lies in a society's willingness and ability to provide the libraries necessary to do that work and the librarians committed to that mission. There is no bottom line more important than the bottom line of democratic self-government.

So watch out for this third culture, these marketeers. Fight their excesses. Never let them talk you into privatizing library services.

Get political. Sharpen up your skills and arguments for convincing voters that while it is painful, taxation is the only way to fully and properly support public libraries, to secure the right to know.

When the idea that you can constantly cut taxes takes over, as it has in the United States, you lose services, you lose educational opportunity, you lose library hours and programs and services, and ultimately libraries. You lose huge institutions from the great society it took decades to build.

When the stink of corruption unfairly envelops all of government, as it has done with Rubbergate, and citizens are newly suspicious of libraries along with other government agencies, we have new trouble.

Even when times are as tough for government as they are now, don't let a few yuppie consumers, a few ruthless entrepreneurs, a few tax rebels, or a few right-wing politicians tell you to run the library as a business. Never let them manage your libraries into market operations that live or die on the fickle fads of the U.S. consumer.

Never let a few antigovernment demagogues convince you that libraries, getting less than one percent of the cost, are as corrupt as Defense, or the House, or the White House, or the statehouse. Libraries are clean and cheap, the best bargain in the United States, public or private sector.

The message is this: We must rediscover the fact that libraries are, must be, public goods, because they meet public needs.

The most important lesson of the last century (and libraries were crucial to our learning that lesson) was learned because we found how to communicate across social, cultural, political, national, religious, and even cold and hot war borders and barriers. The most important lesson we learned was that the more we share information, the better things work.

The lesson of this century, of all history that went before, has been that whether or not anyone makes money doing it, sharing information, having free access to information, work better than their opposite.

You need government for that. The lesson is that whenever any citizen of our nation and world is better informed, everybody benefits.

Are the people well enough informed—informed enough to find work and positive leisure, educated enough to enjoy life, informed enough to engage in the pursuit of happiness? Most important, are the people well enough informed to govern themselves intelligently?

Is the people's right to know secure? That, of course, is the only bottom line, the only appropriate measure, output, or input, for libraries and librarians.

A New Way of Thinking about Librarians

Carla D. Hayden

"The library profession is a profession that is informed, transformed, illuminated, radiated by a fierce and beautiful love of books. A love so overwhelming that it engulfs community after community and makes the culture of our time distinctive, individual, creative, and truly of a spirit."

Now we may smile or sigh or even snicker at that impassioned definition by one of the early library leaders, Francis Clark Sayre, but the time has surely come to think about our profession and what we are. Many of you know and love books and reading, and that fact probably had a great influence on your choice of career. It certainly did for me. Thinking about who we are and why does not negate that love nor diminish it. But being a reader also does not translate into professional capabilities or responsibilities. The state of the book, reading, and information are very much on our minds for professional reasons. The book has endured as a vehicle of communication, mainly because of the previously slow rate of development of a technological replacement and a learned cultural bias toward that replacement, which will probably continue for some time. In further defense of the book, it has been noted that it neither blinks, nor malfunctions, and, almost alone among man-made objects, it does not cause a disease.

Books have certainly engendered a fond memory and a cultural attachment to them as messengers, which has resulted in a public perception, vague though it may be, of libraries as educational storehouses of enlightenment and culture. Yet, as we approach a new century, which is actually similar and sweet to Sayre's time in library history, we may need to look more outward and to think about the larger issues of the role and function of librarians in a rapidly changing society, instead of just focusing on our immediate situations. The current pressing and distressing economic times certainly contribute to this reconsideration and concern about the public's and the policymakers' perceptions about us. Retrenchment and cutbacks are certainly realities with which we must deal.

However, these conditions are taking place within a much larger global and societal context, which may force us to do more serious thinking about our roles. At the same time, as we try to struggle through and survive the immediate crisis, the danger, as Lewis Carroll outlined in *Alice in Wonderland*, is that "if you don't know where you're going to, you will end up somewhere else."

In addition, we may need to think about our roles in the context of our own history. So rather than proposing a new way of thinking about librarians, this is actually a call to reflect and consider, with a series of questions that have a definite place in a conference that asks us to make it happen. That something to make happen is the people's right to know. My remarks will focus primarily on the public arena.

Every major change in society and transformation of

knowledge have produced change in libraries. The role of the librarian has usually related to the prevailing purpose of the institution in that context. A basic definition of library purpose that has evolved is "to provide a service of materials, information, technology, and other services using all of the above, for a clientele based on the environment of the institution," for example, academic settings and businesses.

Librarians and most libraries in the public sector have moved from cultural to educational to social activities in fulfilling their purpose during this century and before. In the late 1800s, when public libraries first came into existence as we would recognize them today, their primary purpose was to uplift and help cultivate the masses. Libraries were actually preservers of the prevailing social order. There were serious debates about the need to censor the public's taste in literature, and information provision was not viewed as a central characteristic. In fact, libraries and their materials were viewed as socializing agents.

The subsequent reform movement at the start of this century touched librarians as well. These librarians rapidly aligned themselves with social workers. Libraries were truly social institutions that reached out to the public, especially the new immigrants, who were to be indoctrinated in the American way. An interesting side note is that part of the effort with immigrants included extensive programming and material selection based on the native cultures, which are strikingly similar to some of the multicultural efforts of today.

The later activism and outreach activities in the 1960s and 1970s actually presented traditional library services but just took them outside of the building. Some of our colleagues would say that the same attitudes that motivated librarians at the turn of the century are still motivating them today. And that there is a type of conservatism that seeks to change individuals but not society. There is little argument that many of the things we do today in libraries were started in the early parts of this century and, with slight revisions, continue. Today's basic library service is traditional library service—helping those who want to help themselves and trying to create a demand for what we already do.

Surely, since most of what we currently consider basic service was formed at the beginning of this century, it needs to be reconsidered as we enter a new one. Indeed, we are facing another era of significant and sweeping societal change as we move toward that information- and knowledge-based society. This is not unlike the situation at the other turn of the century, when the profession was relatively new. Society was moving from an agrarian era to an industrial age. However, there's an important difference. This time we are intimately familiar with the environment of change, and we are even part of the movement.

Toffler, in *Power Shift*, describes our current situation as one of "living through one of those exclamation points in history, when the entire structure of human knowledge is once again trembling with change, as the old barriers fall." Already government and businesses need trained and skilled work forces familiar with the information environment. What is increasingly clear is that work now requires higher and higher informational skills, not all job specific, and workers who must be able to get and exchange information. We are not just accumulating more facts; we are totally reorganizing the production and distribution of knowledge and the symbols used to communicate it. We are interrelating data in more ways, giving them context and thus forming them into information. We are assembling chunks of information into larger and larger models and architectures of knowledge, which does imply vast changes in the way we see the world, create wealth, and exercise power. Toffler predicts that these will present baffling new issues about the uses and misuses of information, which will arise to confront society as a whole.

Now this development relates directly to the right to know, amid what's been called an info agenda, which produces a hunger for knowing about a condition, job entitlements, and anything that relates to the public's welfare. The understanding and the control of information and knowledge will undoubtedly become extremely important, as we are moving toward a time when the key objective is to make sure that all citizens, poor and rich alike, are guaranteed access to the widest possible range of media.

Knowledge, which is our traditional domain, may well become a commodity and not a public good. There are those who feel that libraries and librarians are at the vortex of these developments. Our response will have an impact, not only on the future of our profession, but the future of democracy as well.

However, this change in society is, to use the vernacular, right up our alley. And we can either help lead the way or become passive technocrats or merely purveyors of mass media. One speaker on Friday noted that information is like a type of new car or a vehicle, and everyone is looking around for a driver. Since it is our type of vehicle, we should take the wheel. We could become the people entrusted by the public as managers and navigators, not just custodians, but people who truly help sift through these informational mazes. We may even have to inform the public about these mazes and how they need to know certain things. This is a much more activist and proactive approach, with much more outward thinking and emphasis on getting the word out about what libraries can be, especially when the public may not know about its right to know.

Now you may think that activism and outreach were

hallmarks of another era, when idealism ran rampant throughout the profession as well as society. But this would be going out into the community to listen, to learn, and then interpret, direct, and possibly produce the tools and the mechanisms for the people to achieve their right to information and knowledge. Libraries and librarians could pick the role for their institutions depending on their own situations. It has been suggested that trying to turn a library into something other than a provider of knowledge and culture will not increase the community's level of support. It is important for the community to have

pretty soon) the public to use these tools. We may even create support systems to help people support themselves or help themselves.

Some have already suggested that we should focus primarily on this direction and concentrate on instruction and letting people know how to use the tools. Whatever we choose, this would definitely be a return to a situation in which democratic ideas and beliefs in rights make a difference in what we do. This could also possibly make librarians as important as the material. Perhaps questions about status and professionalism would then diminish.

Our children and their families depend on libraries and schools as part of the intellectual infrastructure that will help them develop into productive citizens and help lead America in the competitive world of tomorrow.

Marian Wright Edelman, president,
Children's Defense Fund

---

a library, not so librarians can have jobs, but because knowledge and culture are important to the community. The public might not be interested in those things themselves, but they know they are desirable and somehow a way to combat ignorance and barbarism. Perhaps if librarians are the focus of the right to know—and not in the self-serving way decried by some of our colleagues but as specialists who are charged with determining the type and level of information service—then the public perception of libraries would moderate, and the people would welcome the addition of a truly useful service provider in their community.

The library would become the place where it happens, via the librarian. The librarian in this scenario would be the information specialist who navigates and leads, steers the course, and is viewed as and prepared to be a uniquely qualified person.

As librarians, we long ago accepted the fact that we do not have to know everything in all of the materials that we provide but, rather, where they are, how to get to them, and how they work. This new role would mean that we are not just the providers of a service, which is basically a supply function and very passive, but are more interpreters. We would also need to work for more standardization of interfaces and information skills. Our role then would be to make the information and materials accessible and to empower (which may become a trite verb

What about the people for whom we would navigate? Will this be just as hard a sell as our cultural and educational roles have been? Many assert that part of the problem in libraries may be that we are still serving the ten percent who use us, and those users are still mainly middle class and of a certain characteristic type. Do we really need to try and meet all the information needs of all the people? If so, our budget would have to be as big as that of the Department of Defense, and we, perhaps, would need, in this election year, a cabinet post.

We do need to find out more about why people need certain types of information and how they use it. There are privacy issues with this, but it would help us to know what is more appropriate and could change perceptions about what we do.

The implications for library education are relevant. What type of librarians are we preparing? Will they need more management and political skills to be able to find ways to ensure equitable access to information sources? In spite of fees and costs, should the government actually be paying for this? Librarians would become advocates. We would work more with the communities and more with politicians and government officials to make sure that these services are free.

Does our protection of the right to know also entail determining what people need to know as well as what they want to know? People may want to know certain things, but they may have a greater need for other information. We would determine what type of information and in what format.

It has been said that in established professions, the practitioner supposedly assumes the responsibilities for deciding what is best for the client. Whether or not the client agrees is theoretically not a factor in the profession's decision. Thus a doctor generally does not have to give whatever treatment a patient requests, but has to prescribe whatever treatment he or she thinks is correct. In contrast, librarians have tended to serve the reader. This is more of a hostess syndrome, which Garrison in her book, *Apostles of Culture*, largely attributes to the feminization of our profession.

Here's another intriguing question. Does the right to know mean that librarians who work for the government or businesses engage in unethical practices? Is the right to know perhaps, as someone has suggested, just another desperate attempt to try and save ourselves as librarians? I think not. We are players in this new society of information—at least we like to think we are.

Consider this. In looking at and researching the information age, most of the books about how we are moving to the information society do not mention libraries at all. If you check the indexes, you will not find libraries or librarians mentioned. Will we, as was suggested by Pierce Butler, decades ago, continue to hold tenaciously to a service long after society has so transformed itself as to render that service socially ineffective; for it's not enough to be the busiest beings, so are the ants. The question is, What are we so busy about?

We are a social agency because we work with and for people. We have a responsibility to be reformers, with the ideal of a citizen who will make more informed decisions. Some feel that the first thing we need to do is to break the public's perception of the library as a cultural institution and position ourselves as the people's information public utility. We need to become part of that information infrastructure and emphasize the library's utilitarian nature. The majority of the people still view us as squares or do-gooders and libraries as places for kids and seniors. Is it time to go to marketing, with its negative business connotations? Is it time to really define our purpose? Do we need to be all things to all people?

The true potential for use is not just wishful thinking, although there is more time now for consideration of the function and not the process. These are not new ways of thinking about librarians, but just thinking again. Not in a crisis mode of saving what we already have, but truly looking at whom we currently serve and whether we want to change that or reach others. We have already served a great number of people, and we do perform a valuable service, and we have had an impact on society.

We have a relationship to the preservation and cultural enlightenment of our society. With society's change from industrial to knowledge based, this is truly our time to define the purpose and function of librarians. Should we not, as one librarian has noted, become intellectual ombudsmen, who make judgments about what the public should at least know in order to make better informed judgments on their own? Others have said that this is sort of a fraternalistic attitude, and certainly more political. In taking this stance we could put our purposes at odds with those who would limit access, and we might actually be embarking on a moral crusade.

Others say, "What's the hurry?" The new literacy necessary for a knowledge-based society will undoubtedly go through the other identifiable stages of literacy, starting with specialists, then having wider impact on institutions, to becoming the preferred medium of business, culture, and politics, and finally becoming so persuasive that even the masses will feel they must have it. If all of this is not to be feared anyway, or thought about now, because it is coming regardless of what we think about it; and if that change brought about by technology usually takes place incrementally, and adjustments by society and individuals will evolve naturally, and this probably won't all be realized in our own lifetimes—then why worry?

Without a reliable timetable, I suggest that thinking about and discussing our purpose and roles are important because change is inevitable. Although it is certainly often uncomfortable, we must make choices, even as our profession is struggling on many fronts. We may even learn, as Helen Keller said, "That to keep faces toward change and behave like free spirits in the presence of fate, is strength undefeatable."

Public Action Faces Public Policy

Supporting Our Right to Know

Cesar Chavez

Thank you very much. Yolanda Cuesta thanks you so much for the introduction. We're pleased to be here with you at your conference. We want to thank your president, Patricia Schuman, for the invitation and bring you greetings and best wishes for a successful conference from America's men, women, and children, whose labor feeds all of us three times a day. We're pleased to be here today addressing the librarians of America because you play a major role in our society. We have some experience with your association through one of our organization's volunteers who called upon many librarians throughout the United States, but especially in California, for information in helping us set up a small library for the workers at our headquarters.

We're especially pleased because of President Schuman's Right to Know program and her vocation as an activist for free speech. We, too, are very concerned about free speech, and any time we are confronted with losing that right we thank God for the foresight of those founding fathers who so strongly insisted that it be a right. We know, because we have been victims on numerous occasions of attempts from the courts with all sorts of legal maneuvers, extralegal gimmicks such as unconstitutional court injunctions, ex parte court orders, and frivolous lawsuits to keep us from exercising free speech.

We have been personally arrested over twenty times in California and some in Arizona for insisting on using free speech in front of supermarkets to tell people about the contaminated grapes and the damage that pesticides and their residue can cause consumers and the impact that they have on the workers and their children. In the spring of 1988 in Passaic, New Jersey, two of my granddaughters, nine and eleven years old, were arrested by the Passaic city police on orders from the A&P supermarkets. They were in front of the store telling consumers that the grapes being sold in the store were contaminated with pesticides. The store objected, asked the police to come, and my granddaughters were arrested. They were taken to jail and released when the district attorney had to deal with the issue of prosecution. They went back to the store, and they were arrested again, and they were released again. Officials couldn't make up their minds whether they had a right or not to break the Constitution.

The same experience has been had by many of us. Several months ago in Southern California, in Montebello, we were picketing in front of a grocery store. The Table Grape Commission, the growers, and the farm labor board, which was set up as legislation to protect workers' rights, went all the way across from East Los Angeles to Burbank and got a willing judge to issue an injunction, a very ridiculous injunction that prevented us by court order from telling people in the parking lot not to shop at the store because those grapes were contaminated. But the injunction went a step further. It also prevented our right to talk to people on the public sidewalk. We called the judge and told him that we were not going to abide by the injunction and were ready to be arrested, and we were. The Montebello police came and arrested twelve workers, arrested a couple of the officers of the union, and myself, and we were taken to jail in Montebello. We were processed, and then the Montebello police called the district attorney's office in downtown Los Angeles to get permission to transfer us to the main jail. At that point, the district attorney said that he was not going to prosecute the case because he didn't think he could win it. We were released and immediately went back to the store to picket again and to talk to people. The next day the Table

for it, and you've got to live for it, and you've got to die for it, and every generation has to win it all over again.

In keeping with that freedom and the right to inform and the right to help people know the other side, we've come to ask you to join our boycott. We're asking you to boycott the red grapes and the green grapes and the black grapes. In fact, we're asking you to boycott anything that looks like a grape just to be sure.

The California table grape is the largest food crop in California. Over ten million pounds are used. Pesticides are used in the harvest and in the production of these

---

Defend your local library as if your freedom depended on it.

John Jakes, author

Grape Commission and the growers and the state farm labor board went to the state appellate court in Los Angeles and obtained a broader injunction for the whole state, preventing us from saying anything in front of any store anywhere in California. We selected a store on Pico Boulevard in Santa Monica, and we told them, the court, that we would not abide by the injunction and were ready to be arrested. We let the press and everybody we could know, and hundreds of people came to see the arrest. I walked into the parking lot and began to break the injunction, and I was not arrested, as we were being enjoined but not arrested for almost two years; but the injunction still stays there saying that we do not have the right to freedom of speech.

We have had other people who have been arrested. Our vice president has been arrested forty-two times on the same issue—whether or not we have a right to talk to consumers at the supermarkets to tell them what we know about the pesticides. We have never had a conviction. This has never gone to trial, but it has cost us time in jail, money, and a lot of attorney fees.

The video you just saw is now also legally prohibited to be shown by court order. A local judge in Kern County, where I live, in Bakersfield, issued an order that the film should not be shown. We called him and told him that we were coming to the courthouse with a portable stand to show it, seeking arrest. The good judge died before that happened, but the video is still enjoined. It is available free of charge. We'd like you to place it in your libraries and show it to your friends, to your association meetings, and anyone who would like to see it.

I suppose that that song "Oh Freedom!" applies here. It says in part that freedom, to keep it, you've got to fight

grapes. Out of the seventy-six known restricted pesticides that are used, the government accounting office has estimated that half of them are potential carcinogens. Pesticides are everywhere. Every water well in that valley is now contaminated. There is residue in the streets, in the fields, in the soil, in the air, in the water, in the school yards, in the playgrounds, in the parks—poison that is harming and killing our children. Those pesticides are linked to high rates of cancer, birth deformities, increasing rates of sterility among the work force, low-birth-weight babies, upper-respiratory-tract problems. We estimate that eighty percent of the workers have some sort of skin disease and a frightening rate of miscarriages and even death because of the pesticides.

In the video you saw the family in the little trailer. One of the victims died several weeks ago. She had a nine-year fight with leukemia and finally lost it.

Little Johnny Rodriguez never made it to ten years. He died at age five. The family was so poor that when he died and he was going to be buried, they were burying him in the wrong plot and the cemetery keeper came and insisted they take the body out of the plot and then take it in the back section of the cemetery for the pauper's plot, adding insult to injury.

Then there is my ten-year friend, Felipe Franco, whom you saw in the video, no arms and no hands, not even stumps. I went to see him not long ago, and he was very happy and he wanted to show me what he has learned, because he's now going to school. You have to imagine a little human being without arms or legs, not even stumps. He somehow rolls on the carpet in his front room and gets a paper with his mouth and then gets a pencil and then labors for several minutes to write his name. When he did that, he asked me to pick up the paper, and I showed him, and he said, "Put it down again," because he misspelled his name. To be there watching this little human being, just to imagine—what could I do? What would you do if you did not have any arms or legs?

This is the setting of the situation. It's continuing. We showed you three cancer clusters, but we know there are more. We know there are many more cancer clusters in the valley, but we don't have time or money or the resources to certify them. It is quite a process to certify them and then fight—big, big fight with the structure and

use economic power very effectively to then say "no!" to whatever it is that we don't want to buy, so that the people who are the sellers and producers will then do things right. We've been very successful. In fact, it is because of a public action, because really in America, however many folks we may have, there are enough people still who care, and we've experienced this for over thirty years.

We have gone to the American public with one issue after another, and we always have been supported. You see, in public policy you need a majority to win. In public

---

A people deprived of information about their government and the world around them are constrained by their ignorance. Their choices are limited by what they are permitted to know.

U.S. Sen. Paul Simon (D-Ill.)

---

with the authorities to get them to admit what we already know.

In McFarland, for instance, they've been fighting for over six years, and the state Department of Health still doesn't know what's causing the cancer, but they say "we know it is not pesticides." They don't really know, but they say that. It's the biggest cover-up after Watergate.

Let me talk to you a little bit about our experience. You have to imagine that our work has to be done in settings not only with minorities racially, but with minorities economically, and then with minorities also in terms of unions in rural areas where very few unions exist. Then we're up against the richest, most powerful, most influential industry in California—the agribusiness—and so for years now we've never been able to get things our way. Help [is not practical] through the legislative process, through what we call the public-policy process, because we don't have the influence, we don't have the money, we don't have the wherewithal to do it. So we have done other things. We have done pretty much what Dr. King had to do with the bus boycott and what Gandhi and others so well did; we said that the public action must have a place if public policy falls down.

Let me remind you that public action takes many forms. We have seen the form it took in Los Angeles with the rioting. It can take the form of a revolution, and also it can take a peaceful form, and our form is boycotts. To go through the marketplace and let the marketplace vote is a different kind of vote. The marketplace is where we

policy the polls close at seven o'clock or eight o'clock on Tuesday night, in public policy you need tons of money to do your work, and you also need a majority to win. But in public action you don't. We estimate that if ninety percent of the people who now buy grapes stop buying grapes, this is enough to get those growers to stop using the pesticides, as we did back in 1970 when we won our first boycott. The demand then was what it is today. We wanted the growers to stop using DDT and DDE, the hard pesticides. The growers told us that they couldn't because they absolutely could not raise any grapes without DDT. In 1970 when they could not sell their grapes, they agreed not to use the DDT, and there are more grapes now than there were when those pesticides were used, and we've got to do the same thing today.

When you go to the store, every time you go by the grapes and don't buy them, you are voting. You don't need a majority to win. If you happen to live by a store that's open twenty-four hours a day, you can also vote twenty-four hours a day—because the votes never close. We say this because we (especially with our friends in the environmental movement) have got to start doing something other than trying to influence the politicians who are caught up in this business of benefit and risk. As you saw, the fellow from the government said, "We've got to balance things and we've got to see what risks we are willing to accept and for what benefits." What this means is that the benefits are the harmful pesticides that the industry can use, and the risk is us.

Perhaps the best story on that is this U.S. Senate discussion about two years ago on clean air—a big debate about what is clean air. But we know what clean air is. Anybody can know that, but they didn't. They finally decided that clean air is anywhere where you get less than one death per every twenty thousand people—that's clean air. I think it's a lot of hot air. What are they doing? They're playing around with the risk-benefit syndrome. When you go to the marketplace, politicians and growers don't have that option. You take that option away from them because you don't have the politicians trying to broker for you.

I'll ask you once again to join us. You can do a lot. Believe me, we know more about boycotts than almost anyone in this country today. We've been at it for thirty years, and it does work, and it's working again. When it does work, they will not use the carcinogens, what you saw in the video. They will stop because we now know that grapes can be grown without harmful pesticides, and the killing and the maiming of our people can be stopped. You can play a major role by just simply not buying the grapes. That's how simple it is. It's so simple that many people can't understand that it does work, but it does.

Let me leave you with this thought. There's a terrible irony. Today, we produce more food in this country than anywhere in the world at any time in the history of the world. Yet the men, women, and children who produce the grapes and the fruits and the dairy products and everything that we eat three times a day oftentimes go hungry. Isn't that a terrible irony? How can they produce food and not be able to have enough to eat themselves? That's what this fight is all about.

Questions and Answers

Q. *Why the tactic of using the marketplace and boycotts? Why not lawsuits, given that the pesticides are so dangerous?*
A. There have been several lawsuits lost. A lawsuit we're involved in cost over half a million dollars, and we lost it because most of the scientists and expert witnesses are not on our side today. So when we go to a court, we don't have either the money or the specialists as court witnesses on our side. Besides, we must understand. See, these courts take place in the valley where the judges and anything that happens pretty much are controlled by agriculture or they're beholden to agriculture or they're in a place where they're subjected to a lot of pressure. We have not won. There have been some minor suits. We're pretty much in the same boat that people were some years back when they were trying to bring suits on asbestos. In the early days, they couldn't win the suits, and it wasn't

until much later that they were able to win. Today, one out of every fifty suits may be won. They are there, but not very effective yet.

Q. [Inaudible]
A. Let me tell you. In 1970, we cleaned grapes from the dreaded DDT pesticides. In so doing, we also then were able to get better working conditions for workers. It was a whole industry. That's our method of doing it, and that's what we've decided. You see, there are two things involved here. It's the conditions of the workers plus the pesticides, and so we need to do both, and the best that we found is through economic pressure where we know we'll win. There's no doubt about it, but it takes time, but it's there. However powerful, the agribusiness cannot influence the American people or at least enough of them to keep us from winning. That's been our strategy, and it's been winnable.

Q. *Are the grapes grown for wine also? Are they also getting the pesticides?*
A. Actually, there are three industries in grapes as you know—the wine, the raisin, and the table grape. The wine grape and the raisin grape, although they also get their share of pesticides, are not subjected to what we argue is the overuse of pesticides, because of the cosmetic effect on the fresh grape that goes to the consumer. The wine grape the consumer doesn't see, and by the time the raisin gets to you it doesn't really matter because it's all shriveled up and doesn't have to look pretty, and so that's the reason. That's why in the table-grape vineyards more than half of all the job-related illnesses are reported from the table-grape industry. More than half of all the crops in California. That's pretty significant.

Q. *What about white grape juice?*
A. We call it juice grape, which is something like wine grape. They have pesticides, but they don't have as much because they're not concerned with the cosmetic effect.

Q. *Question relating to an organic grower.*
A. A good thing you mentioned that name. We don't think that his grapes are really organic. We don't think that because we have seen and heard witness of people who are cutting those grapes with organic labels, but cutting from fields that we very much doubt are organic. He raises both grapes—both organic and nonorganic. We say, just to be sure, those organic grapes, no. Now, the organic grapes that come from the truly organic growers, the small, noncommercial growers, the family-type farms, you have a better chance with them than you would with a large corporation trying to make us believe that everything grows organic, when we know that not everything is organic.

David Martinez, our secretary-treasurer, did an investigation where he saw both boxes—organic label boxes and nonorganic boxes—being picked and packed from the same vineyard, from the same vine, and some were going to organic and some to nonorganic. We took pictures, and we have witnesses of that, so be careful with that kind of gimmick.

Q. *What about grapes from Chile?*
A. Yes, just to be safe. Remember that Chilean grapes have even more pesticides than American grapes because

demand. If there was consumer demand, we would have organic produce on the table tomorrow—everything. There's no demand from the consumer. The National Academy of Sciences in the report of November 1990, I believe, flatly says we've got to encourage the growing community, the growers to grow more organic because the pesticide-grown products are harming not only the consumers, but also the environment. So it's moving that way. In fact, the Academy of Sciences is pressuring the state universities, asking the agricultural departments to begin to get growers to start moving toward the natural

---

In twenty-five years, federal funding for libraries totals less than the cost of one aircraft carrier *(about $3.5 billion).*

---

over there the DDT is not illegal like it is in this country. But let me tell you, there is an agreement between the California grape growers, and that's where all the grapes are grown in the United States, and Chilean grapes, by some kind of an agreement, stop coming to the country by April 15, and then from there on the American grape takes over until December 15. So that from April 15 to December 15 the only grapes in the United States are really American grapes. But they say that because of our boycott? You'll see how grapes are. The grapes are very inexpensive in California, thirty-nine cents a pound right now. In the beginning of the season, generally they are over one dollar, so that's the impact of the boycott on them.

Q. *Isn't there likely to be scarcity with organic products?*
A. No, not really. There are now very reputable scientists who are saying that almost everything can be grown organically. The reason it's not is because there's no

way of growing things. Remember, not too long ago we did not use pesticides and were able to do it for years. For instance, the best wines in the world were grown even before pesticides were around for hundreds of years, so it can be done. Let me just give you one more fact here that's very important to us who are concerned about winning the boycott. We started the boycott, announced the boycott in 1984, in July, and the per capita consumption was almost eight pounds. Today, the per capita consumption is a little bit over six pounds. So we've cut the per capita consumption by two pounds in the United States, and that's very significant. When we started boycotting the grapes, New York, San Francisco, Chicago, Philadelphia, Boston, and Toronto were in that order in terms of the most grapes sold. Today, it's New York, Los Angeles, and Hong Kong. Hong Kong is the third city in the world buying and selling American grapes. They're going there because they're having a hard time selling them here.

Getting the Message Out

Susan Silk

I am here to share with you tips on how to get the message out. This is a topic that I, as a media consultant, love discussing.

First, there need to be some ground rules. Let us all agree that the "out" we mean is beyond this room, beyond librarians, beyond libraries, beyond library journals. "Out" means communicating beyond the professional meeting and beyond the already converted.

"Out" means taking your powerful message to the outside world. It means taking it to those people who may not have stepped inside a library since school but who decide on the state budget for libraries. It means taking it to those individuals who decide on the future funding for librarian education, taking it to those who vote on federal legislation to curtail governmental printing. That's "out" to me.

Without the microphone on this podium, only those people in the very front of this large room would be able to hear me. If I were to emote well, and speak right up, perhaps I could increase my audience and my chances of being heard by a few more people. I would never be heard by the folks in the sixth row, and the back of the room would not even see me. Half the message would be gone, because, at the very least, my presence would be a dot on the distant horizon. They would hear and see nothing.

In fact, without this microphone the vast majority of you would not hear a word I am saying. And if I had something important to say—for example, "Our library is in serious trouble and there won't be enough money

to . . ." or "Censorship is threatening the right of our young children to read"—my failure to be heard could jeopardize the future of an institution that makes the United States unique in the world: a system of public, school, academic, and special libraries that are accessible, available, and affordable.

That microphone is a metaphor for any medium that allows you to be heard beyond the sound of your own voice, to reach an audience more distant from you than the top of your lungs. And should my voice carry well enough to be heard by those in the middle of the room and my content, my remarks, be so unremarkable, so uncompelling as to fail to motivate the audience to action, we have, as they say in the movies, a failure to communicate.

The Shape of the Message

I would like to share with you a few tips on how to shape a compelling message and how to reach out beyond your profession to ensure that your message will be heard. Let us start at the very beginning.

Step number one is the development of a powerful message. In order to create a powerful message, gather around you three or four creative people. Too large a group will be counterproductive. Too small a group will fail to develop the creativity needed. Ask yourselves a series of questions beginning with the obvious: What is the issue? Or, What are we trying to say?

Every issue demands its own message. Do not try to create a compelling message that addresses many issues—the right to know, literacy, censorship, or funding. Each of these is an issue. And each deserves its own message.

As an example, let us take the issue you have decided to address as the threat of censorship to the right to know. Your institution and its professional staff want to fight censorship in your community, and that community can be a neighborhood, an entire town, a high school, or a college campus.

Next you must define your goals in discussing this issue. Do you want more parents to know about the censorship threat and demand a halt at a governmental meeting? Do you want to empower librarians and staff to withstand the pressure of censorship? Do you want to educate the public to the isolated struggle of librarians to fight censorship and the need for public support? Do you want those most negatively impacted by censorship to help educate those who could influence this public-policy decision? There must be consensus on the goal or goals. You must be sure that goals are not in conflict with one another.

Let us suppose for the sake of this discussion that the goals decided upon are these: to tell the public that censorship puts their right to know at risk and to let the public know that librarians are fighting censorship and the public must get involved.

With these goals in mind, kick around ideas for a theme or message. Something short and sweet and to the point. How about librarians and you fighting for the right to read? This message tells me that there is a need to fight for the right to read; it implies that the right to read is at risk and that librarians need my help.

Reaching an Audience

After you have a defined message that will help you achieve specific goals, step number two is to define your audiences. Who will be most adversely affected by the censorship involved? Students? Parents? Then the students and their parents must be identified as victims of the censorship. Who else? Faculty members? If this is a freedom-to-teach issue, then remember that all teachers, and labor unions representing them, are members of your target audience as well.

It is imperative before you begin an external communication program that you know to whom you must speak or reach out and what you want them to hear and why. Why do you need to identify audiences to be reached? Simple—a clear understanding of your

audiences lets you target accurately the various media for your message.

Where to Deliver Your Message

Sixty percent of the population of the United States reportedly gets all or nearly all of its information from the electronic media. Yet we also know that community and governmental leaders are most likely to be part of that forty percent who are still reading for their news and information.

Professional working parents and union officials may attend luncheon meetings or be involved with a professional, civic, or fraternal organization where they might be able to hear you speak during a luncheon, if you were on the program. Students, depending on age, may get information from the school newspaper, campus radio station, or posters located in strategic locations.

With limited time and resources, it is imperative that when you speak directly to a group—at a luncheon meeting, for example—the audience you need to reach is hearing you. With limited time and resources, whenever you take the time to secure a media interview you must know that the audiences being reached contain members of the target group that you have identified. The only way to ensure that your compelling message reaches the right target is to know who that target audience is and from where they receive information.

Seeking Public-Speaking Opportunities

If your anticensorship campaign has set as its goal the passage of state legislation banning censorship, then influencing public policy, getting the legislature to pass that legislation, can be aided in a number of ways. One way is directly through speaking before a legislative committee on the risks of censorship.

The legislative audience may also be reached indirectly in a couple of ways. For example, by speaking to groups of impacted citizens and urging them to contact their state legislators, you can send a powerful message to those legislators.

Which citizens are most adversely affected by the threatened censorship? Contact parent-teacher associations, civic and fraternal organizations, the Rotary and Kiwanis clubs, the chamber of commerce, trade and professional associations, and any others that you think your message will appeal to enough so that they get out and fight for it. Ask for an opportunity to speak to their membership about a problem, fast becoming a crisis that is impacting their membership. You will be surprised at how rapidly they can fit you into the schedule.

Be sure, as you prepare your remarks, that you remember that you want to ask the audience to do something—to write to their state representatives and senators. Be sure to urge letter writing at least twice during the speech. You might also come prepared with preprinted postcards to hand out after your remarks.

Begin now to make a list of the wide variety of groups in your community that you might speak to about different topics. Just be sure that the audience is appropriate for the message you intend to deliver!

The legislative audience may also be contacted indirectly by taking advantage of the mass media to reach a broad audience and urging this broad audience to write to these elected state officials.

Using the Mass Media to Get Your Message Across

Influencing public policy through the use of mass media requires time and practice, but it need not be mysterious. In dealing with the mass media, remember that the media are driven by news or the illusion of news.

The mass media, because of their broad audience, must do stories that appeal to a broad audience. With your target audience or audiences in mind, be selective about what mass media outlets you approach to tell your story.

Call the sales departments at any mass media outlet and ask to be sent an advertising packet so that you know who is reading, listening to, or viewing the outlet. Match this information against what you already know about your target audiences. By being media savvy in this way, you are acting as a matchmaker!

The mass media, and especially the electronic media—television (broadcast and narrowcast, or cable) and radio—due to their nature, are forced to reduce complex stories to easy-to-understand stories. You must be able to explain your story in people terms: in terms of problems and solutions or good and evil. In addition, the mass media are unpredictable. Be prepared to do media interviews when they need you, which might not be when it is most convenient to you!

There are four steps I recommend to volunteers preparing to reach out to the mass media:

1. Write a one-page letter to reporters, editors, and producers suggesting that the threat to the public's right to know is impacting their audience or readership.
2. After the letter is mailed and with enough time allowed for delivery, contact by telephone these same reporters, editors, and producers to determine interest in the story. Do not be surprised if during this telephone conversation you are asked to send additional information or to provide examples in your community of tangible ways that the right to know is being threatened.
3. You may need to call reporters, editors, and producers several times to reach them, provide all the background information needed, before you get a commitment to do an interview or a story on the subject.
4. When the interview occurs, be sure that you strongly state your message over and over again so that the reporter and/or the audience hears you!

It is imperative to remember that doing media relations work gets easier with experience, and being a spokesperson becomes fun over time. Remember also that most novice spokespeople are apprehensive if not downright terrified the first time they speak up. We all become stronger, clearer, and more convincing speakers with practice.

Conclusions

Getting the message out to nonlibrarians is imperative if librarians are to be valued in our society. Getting the message out to a nonlibrarian audience is imperative if the American Library Association is to be effective in its fight for the principles of the library profession and everything that librarians, libraries, and librarianship stand for in our society.

During the past two years we have begun to move the American Library Association and, more important, librarians to the front of the consciousness of Americans. A speakers' bureau of nearly seventy volunteers has been created, trained, and introduced to the media. An aggressive, proactive media relations program has created mass media opportunities for the ALA leadership and volunteer spokespeople across the country. Editorials, op-ed pages, radio, television, and newspaper feature and news stories have been appearing all over the country for the past year.

Most recently, nearly a hundred thousand citizens called an 800 number to show their support for the important role that libraries play in society. Thousands of Americans willing to take the time registered their support. Each of those calls translates to power—power to influence federal legislation, power to influence local government. No matter the issue, librarians—the preservers and protectors of our right to know—will always have a powerful message. You must continue to be proactive, you must continue to speak up, and you must continue to speak out.

The Call to Action

Charles E. Beard

Technology and the knowledge explosion have propelled even the smallest libraries into the unenviable position of attempting to meet the public's demand for universal, instantaneous, detailed information. Once today's children begin to communicate verbally, to respond visually, to read, and to write, their demands for answers become almost insatiable. This basic need for information and knowledge continues throughout the child's lifetime. Library users, especially those who pay taxes, expect librarians, the collectors, disseminators, and interpreters of accumulated knowledge to meet their information needs whenever they enter a library, whether it is in person or via a computer. Our library patrons expect to receive prompt assistance from whatever library they might choose to use. They resent being referred back to the library that has traditionally served them.

Librarians are information providers. We have waited for generations to be acknowledged as central players in the world of education and learning. To be fully accepted in this role each of us must be prepared to provide patrons free access to the world's recorded knowledge. Our profession has been very slow to recognize that we cannot provide all these resources in "splendid isolation," but only through carefully planned and constructed coalitions with other libraries, agencies, institutions, and organizations. While librarians are developing more partnerships and cooperatives, they must be strengthened and replicated if we are to assure equitable library ser-vices for everyone in our country, whether rich or poor, black or white, literate or illiterate, young or old. We must accept the fact that school, public, and academic libraries have to be equal players in this endeavor, and we must also give more than lip service to the concept that public, school, and academic libraries provide the same services and share common goals. Briefly, let us look at some of the most important alliances that we must establish if libraries are to reach their full service potential. I have chosen examples that can be easily tailored, expanded, and duplicated, that aren't expensive to implement, and that appeal to librarians everywhere in any size town or city.

The American Library Association's recent Call for America's Libraries: Say Yes to Your Right to Know campaign is a prime example of a viable library public relations campaign that succeeded because ALA's staff and members throughout the country made a concentrated effort to work with the media. Thanks to many of you who participated in the media-training workshop and became members of ALA's Speakers' Network, hundreds of media interviews reached millions of Americans. Your efforts snowballed into unbelievable media coverage of the financial plight of America's libraries with editorials in the *New York Times*, *USA Today*, the *Christian Science Monitor*, and untold numbers of articles in other newspapers throughout the country. A true highlight of our media blitz was the PBS news commentary "Washington Week in Review," which presented an impressive, impassioned dialogue on the crisis in library funding. Virtually every major radio network, including the Associated Press, United Press International, ABC, and the Independent Broadcasters Network, carried interviews with the ALA president, Patricia Glass Schuman. This national coverage about libraries and our hard times would not have been possible without librarians working in continuous daily contact with the news media. The campaign also generated the names and addresses of 75,743 library supporters from across the country to whom we can now turn when we need support for library projects and advo-

assisted. Of almost equal importance to the furtherance of our political position are the partnerships we develop with public-policy groups such as the League of Women Voters and environmental groups. Libraries must receive more funding from every governmental level if we are to provide services and resources for our respective clienteles. Librarians can only affect this additional funding by creating the correct political alliances.

Of major concern to all educated Americans is the ever-increasing illiteracy problem among our country's population. In Georgia, twenty percent of our eighteen-

---

Libraries save business leaders, scientists, and engineers an estimated $19 billion a year in information resources.

---

cacy. The petition campaign that followed has added another 222,000 names and addresses. Of even greater importance are the untold millions of Americans who have been reminded of how important libraries are to their daily lives. The Call for America's Libraries campaign represents millions of dollars in library publicity that actually cost the association nothing. Less than $100,000 in donated funds from our committed vendors was spent. Librarians across the United States made it happen!

Libraries enjoy an unsullied reputation as the country's best bargain. Librarians are renowned for the services and resources we provide while expending so few tax dollars. To be exact, less than $15.60 is spent per capita by all of our nation's publicly supported libraries. Public libraries today serve sixty-six percent of America's population for less than one percent of the total tax dollars collected by all levels of government. All our public relations programs should be designed to inform public officials of the library's ability to serve every segment of the population without spending tremendous sums of money. One way to show the decision makers what a bargain libraries are is to offer specific services to local county and city officials. Obviously politicians will respond more favorably to requests from librarians who have done them favors and developed information programs and offered reference assistance to enable them to more effectively serve their constituents. Not enough of us think about making such an offer, much less take the time to establish such a positive beneficial relationship with local policymakers even as our budgets are being slashed. You can be sure the library's help as well as its bargain status will be remembered when budgets are being developed by these very same lawmakers we have

year-olds are functionally illiterate. Probably the situation is similar in your state if numbers of adolescents and adults lack the very basic reading and comprehension skills. Every social agency that is attempting to solve this insidious, growing problem is looking for partners who can assist in remedying this national dilemma. Examples of successful coalitions involving libraries and literacy groups exist everywhere, but one of the best can be found in the Atlanta metropolitan area. The DeKalb Public Library System has developed an intergenerational literacy program that introduces very young children (birth to thirty-six months) to early skills while simultaneously improving the parent's reading, writing, and literacy skills. The target group is teenage mothers, ages sixteen to nineteen years old, who have dropped out of school and are poor readers, usually economically deprived, and are obviously not well equipped to provide learning experiences for their infants. Six-week sessions offer twelve hours of intergenerational instruction, with forty-five minutes play-with-a-purpose segments to ensure the development of early learning skills for the offspring. This program evolved through the library's coalition with the Literacy Volunteers of America and a local child-development center. A similar program has been designed in cooperation with several literacy agencies and the Jacksonville, Florida/Duvall County Public Library System. Even more unique is the citywide literacy program developed and managed by the University of New Mexico in cooperation with four local literacy centers.

Extensive research has proven that participants in literacy programs see the library as a nonthreatening environment that does not call attention to their need for special help. This fact alone coupled with our expertise and commitment to teaching reading and developing comprehension skills should ensure our successful and equal participation in any literacy venture. The time has come for every library in the country to become involved in some type of local literacy effort if we as a nation are going to control and begin to substantially reduce illiteracy in the foreseeable future.

Welfare agencies are always seeking organizations and agencies to assist in developing services for Americans living in poverty. One of their most sought-after partners has always been our libraries, because they offer well-developed educational and informational com-

the local libraries and these book-discussion clubs have continued. In some instances they have been joined by other civic and professional groups to become more formalized Friends of the Library organizations. Unfortunately, in other communities we have allowed this very natural supportive alliance to become dormant because library administrators have not nurtured the relationship. Today, our most service-oriented, as well as our wealthiest, organizations are professional and civic clubs, e.g., Rotary, Kiwanis, Association of University Professors and University Women, Pilot, Business and

---

Research shows the public library is the most important institution in helping children retain learning skills during the summer months.

---

ponents. Libraries, and librarians in turn, benefit from coalitions with welfare providers because we learn better advocacy techniques from them, we oftentimes can share expenses and/or receive supplemental funding from these agencies, and we easily create significant goodwill in our community as the word spreads of free library services to the very poorest neighborhoods in our towns and cities. Library deliveries in conjunction with Meals on Wheels, volunteer reading programs in nursing homes that admit Medicaid patients (such as the program organized by the Westchester Library System), as well as summer reading programs everywhere for children and young people whose families are on welfare, are just a few examples of the types of library/social service coalitions that serve our community's economically underprivileged populations. Project Homeless, which provides read-aloud sessions for children and parents alike and responds to the needs of children ages two to thirteen in the homeless shelters of DeKalb County, Georgia, is an even more unique approach to serving our country's poor. Certainly with the recent unrest in Los Angeles, Atlanta, and many other cities, we have been painfully reminded once again of the increasing gap between America's haves and have-nots and of our profession's special commitment to providing information and learning for those who can afford to pay nothing. Librarians must continue to develop these coalitions with social agencies if we are truly committed to serve the economically deprived more effectively.

The libraries in our country, whether subscription or public, were usually begun and oftentimes largely supported in their earliest years by literary societies or book clubs. In many towns and cities, relationships between

Professional Women, and book clubs that have traditionally supported libraries. All of these groups are continuously reassessing their worthy causes, emphasizing those that benefit the community and their own club interests. While book clubs are obviously a natural library friend, other civic groups have proven to be just as supportive if they are informed about library services and encouraged to work with us.

A small town in Alabama has had an Apple Annie/Arts and Crafts Show for years that is cosponsored by the Friends of the Library and a local book club with help from the library staff. It is a fund-raiser for all three groups. Recently the two clubs voted to give the library every penny of the profit from the annual event. Last year the event generated enough money to ensure that the library would have a substantial contingency fund for the first time in its history. With last year's economic situation, it could not have come at a better time.

We must begin to seek more funding from civic groups and other community organizations through these types of arrangements if we expect to meet all the demands of our various publics. Since gifts provided from all donors average only about eleven percent of all dollars spent on libraries, librarians must still be prepared to continue lobbying for substantial increases from all levels of government.

One of the most politically influential and affluent segments of any municipality is its business and industrial sector. Some library decision makers have shied away from reciprocal arrangements with business and industry. Instead of encouraging businesses' considerable political support in exchange for specialized library services that enhance their day-to-day operations, as well as their planning and research, most of us have chosen to ignore their need for service. Whether we offer simple reference assistance or more complex packaged information, some coalitions between libraries and businesses do exist. One of the most exciting is the Long Island Business and Educational Partnership. This cooperative includes public libraries, industries and businesses, universities and colleges, as well as their respective libraries, who share resources and information to solve economic and educational problems in that very populous area of New York State. I am convinced that libraries must commit the resources in staff, material, and services to meet local business-information exigencies. The library community could certainly use the political support and financial backing from the business sector that I believe would be naturally forthcoming if these mutually supportive arrangements became realities.

The last coalitions are the most important, and yet in many areas of the United States, library coalitions have become the most difficult to achieve. Cooperatives among libraries working toward a common goal, whether it be resource sharing, combined operations, simple referrals, or advocacy coalitions, have not flourished as universally as they should have in this country. Even more alarming is the fact that some libraries have refused to develop local library-service-program cooperatives to the extent that everyone in their community receives an acceptable level of library service. Unfortunately, the attitude still persists among many of us that if a media center gets more funding, then the local college library will get less, or if a public and a college library combine operations, the policymakers will decide that we don't need both types of libraries anymore, or if we librarians borrow materials extensively from other nearby libraries, our library's acquisitions budget will be significantly reduced. To the contrary, resource-sharing coalitions utilizing the very latest technological developments are enhancing every member library's ability to serve users, sometimes at a reduced cost.

In Michigan, M-Link connects the University of Michigan Library with seven rural public libraries to provide a business data online and referral service to encourage the continued economic development of agricultural areas. Every participant is receiving more financial support from its respective administrator because every segment of the community is being better served. Technology is truly revolutionizing our ability to serve the user population more economically and more efficiently.

A coalition of public, school, and academic libraries was officially organized in 1986 when Georgia's SOLINET members agreed to participate in GOLD (Georgia On-Line Database) and create a state catalog.

SOLINET, the southeastern bibliographic utility, consolidated the records of its participating members and all nonmembers who were willing to pay a minimal fee to input their bibliographic records into the union list for Georgia's libraries. GOLD is already equalizing information access in the rural areas and has proven to be an immediate coalition success story.

Wheeler County High, a rural school with an enrollment of five hundred students, recently won state and national honors in the 1991 History Contest by utilizing interlibrary loan and GOLD. In preparation for the competition, the students found ten of the required eighty-three sources in their media center and local public library. The other seventy-three were located via GOLD and borrowed through the regional public library's interlibrary-loan service. The small school media center only subscribed to fifteen journals and actually owned fewer than four thousand books. The Georgia librarians who plan our annual state library legislative day immediately recognized the public relations value of inviting the members of Wheeler's winning team to talk about the contest and GOLD during the legislative-day luncheon. The legislators were so impressed that both the Georgia house and the senate passed resolutions praising the students and the GOLD connection. A delegation of librarians and students also met with the governor during the day's festivities and discussed the value of Georgia's library database. As a result, funding for the expansion of GOLD has been promised for the future.

Library cooperatives do not have to involve an expensive investment in software, hardware, or personnel. Coalitions can be implemented quite inexpensively if librarians are willing to think of the public's need before our personal convenience and to work a little harder and if librarians are committed philosophically to working together as equals. Carrollton, Georgia, which is located about fifty miles from Atlanta, is the home of the West Georgia Public Library System Headquarters as well as my college. The public library serves a five-county area, one-fourth suburban and three-fourths rural. The library's courier service not only delivers materials to the public library branches in all five counties twice a week but also to every school media center that has requested any items. If the public library system doesn't have the resource requested, then the college library provides the book or article. All materials are circulated gratis by the libraries involved, even when articles must be photocopied or faxed. For years the college's academic community and the public library users have been encouraged to use both collections by simply presenting their respective borrowers' cards. Schoolchildren of all ages are encouraged to use the public library for certain materials, and those in middle school or older are welcomed at the college library to research other projects. Because of this history of cooperation, when the city high school's new media center begins operation this fall, with all the latest technical equipment and electronic databases that neither the college nor the public library own, it will be open to everyone. Fortunately for all of us, plans are underway to connect the college library, the public library headquarters, and the high school media center via fiber-optic cable to further enhance our resource-sharing efforts. You can be sure that all of us are very quick to remind our bosses of how much we are saving by sharing our resources and

Recently there has been dramatic growth in multitype library networks, consortia, and cooperative services. Unfortunately one finds fewer examples of active coalition building on the part of individual libraries, especially those that are located in smaller, isolated communities. Librarians in small towns and in many cities do not appear to be oriented toward actively reaching out to and working effectively with other organized groups or institutions. We must be more aggressive and take an active initiating role in coalition building, even though this

---

It won't matter that I set the NFL record if twenty years from now, kids can't go to the library and read in a book what I did.

Derrick Thomas, linebacker for the Kansas
City Chiefs, NFL Defensive Player
of the Year, and Library Hero

---

establishing even these limited areas of acquisition responsibility through our local library coalition.

Four years ago West Georgia College established its second off-campus center that offers a general-studies curriculum in Newnan, Georgia, a community twenty miles away. The library's goal was to provide an acceptable level of service immediately; yet it had an annual library budget of only $20,000 for materials, library staff, and equipment. Newnan, however, had a newly built public library building. The public library director and I agreed, after some discussion, to join forces to better serve both the general public and the West Georgia College community. The Newnan Public Library staff, collection, and building are used by the West Georgia College community. West Georgia College, in turn, purchases a substantial number of titles annually and provides the Newnan Library with online access to the card catalog, a fax machine, and a periodical index database. Courier service also operates as needed, providing materials and reference support from West Georgia College's Ingram Library without any differentiation whatsoever between the requests of WGC students and the public library patrons. This cooperative effort has been in existence for three-and-a-half years, and both libraries and their users have benefited greatly. The college's administration and the city have increased funding annually because both "town and gown" users have been so vocal about their satisfaction with this cooperative arrangement.

often goes against the traditional stance of neutrality that we adopted years ago in the interest of representing all sides of an issue equally. We must make the public much more aware of library information resources and services if we are to change the perception that libraries frequently fail to meet the information needs of other potential coalition partners. We must assist these groups in identifying the information they need and also assist them in understanding and interpreting. Coalition building must involve identifying our allies and deciding what will be the mutual basis for joint action. We must be flexible, willing to experiment, and capable of reshaping the parameters of collaborative agreements. We must be able to distinguish between what individuals say, what an organization and movement says, and what our coalition says. Negotiation and renegotiation are inherent to the coalition-building process. We must recognize that it is permissible for participants to agree to disagree. Quite frequently we may agree on only one issue, but as a famous sociologist once wrote, "Coalitions are marriages of convenience, not overpowering romantic couplings." Employing these techniques, we must build better political, social, informational, and literacy coalitions if we are to survive economically.

I challenge you to take an active role in developing the most advantageous coalition possible for your library, keeping in mind the absolute necessity for libraries to provide equitable, free access to information for everyone.

Your Right to Know

The Profession's Response

Compiled by Joseph A. Boisse and Carla Stoffle

The conference-within-a-conference format for an ALA president's program has been used three times in the past fifteen years. Each time the purpose was to allow a large cross section of the profession to explore a critical issue in more depth than is usually the case with a presenter followed by a short question-and-answer period. An important component of the program has been the provision of opportunities for librarians to discuss and delineate further the issues raised by the speakers and the background materials, to identify activities that individual librarians or libraries are engaging in that might be adopted by others, and to develop alternatives for future action for individuals, libraries, and the American Library Association. The reactions and suggestions from the previous programs have been included in the conference publications and have stimulated action beyond the conference both on the local and state scenes and the national scene through the American Library Association.

The "Your Right to Know: Librarians Make It Happen" theme, with its focus on mobilizing the profession and individual librarians to action, is especially well suited for the conference-within-a-conference format. The call to recognize, protect, and expand the right to know is an appeal to grass-roots action and will succeed only if large numbers of librarians are knowledgeable about the issues, have clear direction, accept responsibility, and engage and cooperate with one another and with others of similar values outside the profession.

Over one thousand librarians representing all types of libraries, all sections of the country, all age groups, and all races and ethnic groups answered the call to come together for an entire day and help build on public-awareness activities and better understand the theme that librarians make a difference, promoted by the Rally for America's Libraries. Among the participants were several past presidents of the association, librarians from almost all fifty states, individuals working in all types of libraries, librarians with forty years in the profession, and future librarians still in library school. The gathering truly represented a cross section of our profession. Their preparation for participation was intensive. Every registrant received eight background papers in the spring. These papers, especially commissioned for this program, were designed to help the participants more fully understand the issues addressed by the speakers and to help focus their discussion and suggestions to achieve the goals of the program.

The facilitators and recorders devoted even more time to preparing for this program. They all took part in a special three-hour training session during the 1992 ALA Midwinter Meeting. The purpose of that session was to ensure that good discussions would be facilitated and that participant discussion and suggestions would be accurately and clearly recorded.

The participants arrived at the program early, filled with enthusiasm for the topic. Most stayed the entire day.

Clearly, those in attendance felt they could make a difference in their own libraries and communities. Each came with a commitment to the right to know, and all wanted to learn more about what they could do to protect and expand it.

The registrants were assigned to tables of eight, thus ensuring that each individual would have ample opportunity to be involved in the give-and-take during the discussion periods. Furthermore, the assignments were made so that each table would have the benefit of opinions from librarians from different types of libraries and from different geographical regions.

pants also observed that the public does not know how bad things are in regard to library funding today. The general public also does not understand fully the negative impact created on the availability of information resources by privatization, the commercialization of information (especially government information), and the monopolization of publishing by a few commercial firms. Responsibility for this current state of affairs was assigned to librarians themselves and to the lack of leadership in the profession—library directors most usually: "Until librarians say libraries are in trouble, patrons won't know or act."

Students who attend schools with library school media programs staffed by full-time professionals develop better reading and study skills. . . .When adjusted for inflation, funding for school library media centers is down sixteen percent *in public and* fourteen percent *in private schools over the last decade.*

Two formal discussion periods of one hour each were provided. Additional time for informal discussion was provided during the two twenty-minute breaks and during the one-hour lunch period. Discussion was lively and constant during all these times.

Recorders for the sessions were asked to note participant questions, observations, and suggestions and then to identify or summarize the key points or issues. These notes were then collected at the end of the discussion periods, and what follows is a distillation of these contributions.

The overwhelming reaction to the Right to Know program was that it was long overdue. Participants agreed that there is a right to know and that librarians do and must continue to make it happen. Many commented that in U.S. society librarians are charged with the primary responsibility for ensuring that right is preserved. One participant noted, "The program spoke to my heart." Another said, "Nobody is going to rescue us. I know I have to get more active."

The members of the discussion groups also agreed that there is strong public support for libraries and that people do care about their libraries. The discussants felt that libraries have a huge reservoir of untapped goodwill and that the public does think the library is doing a good job: "People care about libraries. If they know your problems they will support you." However, the partici-

In general, the participants accepted the Hayden characterization of current library services and librarian activities as being in the hostess rather than the navigator mode. There was clear support for librarians moving more to the navigator role and a call for a redefinition of what librarians do. Support was voiced for changing job descriptions and then for ensuring that work activities actually change to reflect accurately the changed descriptions. It was almost unanimous that librarians should be analyzers and interpreters of information and the new information technologies. Education is another area that was identified as a major activity for the librarian. Several tables specified: "Librarians need to focus on education and the empowerment of users"; "Librarians need to provide access so that users can actually get information themselves"; "Librarians need to take responsibility for designing tools that empower users in their information searches."

Participants felt that librarians must become more proactive: "We must be out on the field participating, not in the stands observing." There was also clear agreement that librarians must expand who is served, and participants went on record saying that clearly only a small percentage of the population (regardless of the type of library) is served presently. To be more effective in expanding the user base, the participants identified the need to focus on the customers' needs and perspectives rather than the needs and perspectives of librarians or what librarians think the customer needs.

After agreeing that the role of librarians needs to change, many participants then came to the conclusion that librarians need to be educated differently than they have been or are today. New skills and greater self-esteem are necessary for the profession to succeed. Among the needed skills identified were public relations and political skills. Librarians need to be able to identify or assess community needs; librarians must be able to translate these into programs; then librarians need to be able to describe the needs of the library and the library's new programs in terms that the key political or opinion leaders in the community will understand; librarians need to be able to identify and cultivate allies who will be able to tell the library story and increase support for the library.

The participants also noted: "A different type of person needs to be recruited to the profession" and "The profession must have librarians representing the diversity of the population at large."

While most participants agreed with the observations of John Berry about fees and about the need to take the library out of the economics of the marketplace style of operation and return to the "library as public utility" or "library as a public good," one group expressed the feeling that "Berry raised 101 questions for which there are no answers." The participants strongly agreed with Berry that fees deny the right to know, and the right to know depends on information being available without charge. However, several groups did ask, "What *does* constitute a fee?" In addition, other groups expressed the belief that libraries could learn a lot about improving effectiveness and how to maximize the dollars available from studying current business practices. Many felt that libraries do not make the best use of the resources already available nor had librarians demonstrated they were making tough choices and reallocating to support priorities.

In the opinion of the participants, the presentation by Cesar Chavez best exemplified why the right to know is important and why it must be protected at all costs. Chavez presented clear evidence that the general public is being deprived of information concerning its well-being, even though it has a right to that information. While librarians had worked with the United Farm Workers to get out the information that was available, some participants suggested that this was a specific area where libraries "should have and could have done more." One table found it intriguing and enlightening that the United Farm Workers, "an ethnic minority, as well as an economic and a political minority," were playing the lead role on this important health-information issue.

Ideas for improving the visibility of libraries and for making the public aware of what librarians do were found on virtually every summary of participant discussions.

One group commented, "We need to get out our success stories." Others said, "We must talk about the good things we do and keep that before the public," and "We cannot wait for a problem or crisis to arise to get our story out." Some specific suggestions for "getting the story out" included:

- Putting library materials in welcome-wagon packets
- Writing news articles and press releases based on library success stories on a regular basis
- Preparing radio and TV spots
- Providing information issues or topics for radio call-in shows
- Staging or cosponsoring events with other agencies
- Talking with business leaders about the economic-development contributions the library can make
- Looking for photo opportunities, especially with or for local officials or administrators, and creating such opportunities regularly
- Speaking to businesspeople through Rotary Clubs, the Chamber of Commerce, and other business groups
- Preparing exhibits, displays, and bookmarks that tell the library story and distributing these inside and outside the library
- Attending meetings of local government groups and noting where librarians may be able to provide helpful information on civic issues
- Talking about the library's activities with friends and neighbors and in all informal interactions outside of work
- Having Friends or trustees give talks in the community or asking Friends to arrange for library staff to give talks at key agencies or groups
- Preparing materials to send to new students and faculty

Whatever techniques are used, most participants feel that, to be successful, the library must first clarify its mission, communicate the mission widely (or "let folks know"), make public services a priority, budget for priorities, invest in planning and assessment, develop a long-range plan, and make visibility every staff member's responsibility. Concern was expressed in several groups that staff members have not been empowered and encouraged to promote the library's message on the job and in their personal lives. One group noted, "Awareness starts with us."

Most groups also addressed the question of politics. Many participants felt that librarians must become more politically astute: "Librarians must learn to understand and use the political process." Librarians must be able to speak to political leaders in language they will understand. Librarians should assign staff to work with local government officials, key community leaders, or academic and school administrators to help them see first-hand what librarians can do to help them with their work. Librarians must learn to lobby effectively, or educate legislators and administrators who are in charge of libraries; this can include using influential members of the Friends or board of trustees to tell the library's story. Some participants have held legislative briefings in the library and/or breakfast and luncheon meetings between legislators and librarians sponsored by the Friends.

Many participants concluded that understanding politics and developing and using political skills are important beyond the legislative process. There are influential power brokers in the community that can pro-

the value of outside media experts. Many groups indicated that hiring a P.R. person or a public-information officer should be a high priority for libraries. At a minimum, participants agreed that librarians must identify media leaders, get to know them, and learn how the media works, including schedules, typically slow news days, and what kinds of stories are likely to receive attention. This will increase the likelihood that stories and interviews will be used. Some groups suggested that media messages needed to be targeted to specific audiences to be successful.

Nearly all of the groups addressed the question of

My challenge to you is not just to be noisy, but to be able, as a profession, to knit together for the rest of us a better understanding of the role you [librarians] play across the nation.

U.S. Rep. Newt Gingrich (R-Ga.)

---

vide dollars, other resources, or just moral support. These are important assets, and librarians must be able to cultivate and use these individuals or groups appropriately. Understanding how to contact and sell these individuals on the benefits of the library requires an understanding of their needs, concerns, and language. For example, the business and industrial sectors of the community have much to gain from strong libraries regardless of type. Meeting them on their turf and learning to frame the message in terms of their self-interest is key.

Several groups felt that librarians had to stop their bickering and learn to work together to be more effective politically: "The profession needs unity" and "Librarians from all types of libraries need to work together" and "Fear-of-loss-of-turf mentality creates barriers."

Networking and supporting one another were stressed over and over again, clearly underscoring the importance of the remarks made by Charles Beard. The participants found the Beard examples illustrative and were heartened by the growing cooperation among types of librarians that he pointed out.

The importance of the media, developing good relations with the media, and understanding how to increase media coverage received considerable participant attention. Most commented that the presentation by Susan Silk was extremely helpful. After hearing Silk, several participants declared that they had gained an appreciation for

what the American Library Association should be doing to protect the right to know and to raise public awareness of the dangers currently being faced. Among those mentioned were the following:

- Enter into national coalitions with organizations like the Association for Childhood Education and the International Reading Association
- Quadruple the funding for the Washington Office
- Create and distribute videos like the one shown at the opening session
- Make the phone campaign an annual event
- Continue the call-in and call it Speak Up for America's Libraries
- Network the attendees at this program
- Work with the states but provide more planning time
- Develop continuity from year to year and build on previous themes—don't select a new theme annually

Participants generally ended their comments with "Don't waste this beginning"; "We must continue our momentum"; "It is nice to have ALA becoming a really activist organization getting publicity, please continue"; "Why doesn't ALA do a sequel to their program—'Your Need to Know: Librarians Help You Meet It'?"; "This program got in touch with our passion and we must now translate this to local action."

Models for
Action

Marketing
Your Right to Know
at State and Local Levels

How Librarians Help

Real Stories Found by Students in the Library School Project

Compiled by Joan C. Durrance

Your Right to Know: Librarians Make It Happen" is a powerful slogan. To bring life to it, librarians need to better understand how they do help people get the information they need. An article I wrote for the 1992 President's Program emphasized how important anecdotal information is to a librarian's understanding of the role she plays in assuring the right to know to citizens with widely differing problems and situations.[1] The newly published manual on planning job and career information services shows librarians how to collect these stories.[2]

Librarians who develop services designed to fulfill specific needs (such as literacy programs, outreach services to the elderly, job and career centers, and economic development programs) generally have a storehouse of anecdotal material that shows what their clientele thinks are valuable services. The strength of this kind of material is that it is often in the words of the people who have been assisted. Most people who have been helped are quick to express their gratitude. In the process of expression, they explain how being helped affected their lives.

Librarians find that hearing a story about how they helped someone can influence how they practice. My own files are filled with warm, inspirational stories and anecdotes that have been told about librarians and other staff who work in job and career centers in public libraries. Often these stories are told to the library staff by the

proud users of these services. At job centers they may start out something like "I wanted you to know—I got a job!" Then follow details about how the librarian contributed to getting the job. Sometimes they are told directly to the library director, starting something like "You really ought to be proud of what they are doing at the job center. . . . " They often include details about how the help was valuable as well as expressions of surprise that such a service was available at the library.

This summer, during the Right to Know program I asked Ruth Schwab, a reference librarian whose library includes an education information center, if she could recall how she had helped someone. She thought a moment and recounted this story, which was told to her while she sat in the waiting room of her dentist's office. A woman sitting across from Ms. Schwab while they waited for the dentist tried for some time to figure out how she knew her. They chatted idly about where they might have met until the woman realized who she was. She then exclaimed, "You're the woman who changed my life! You're the librarian!" This was followed by a lengthy recounting of what she had done with her life since the time she had first come to the education information center several years earlier and began working to get her GED (general equivalency diploma, or high school diploma). She had completed the GED and had gone on for further training to become an assistant in a physician's office. She was currently employed in a physician's office and profusely thanked Ms. Schwab for helping her get started in a new, rewarding life.

How librarians help citizens gain their right to know varies considerably. This woman, although she may not have known it at the time she received help at the library, needed to know that through education and training, she could gain access to a better job. That realization came over time. The story shows how the librarian helped her—from her own perspective.

The Library School Project

Librarians who are able to know how they have helped people find librarianship particularly rewarding. The Right to Know (RTK) Committee sought to encourage library school students, while they were enrolled in their professional program, to begin to understand the experience of knowing how a professional helps. The RTK's Library School Project used a technique developed by Professor Sara Fine of the University of Pittsburgh School of Library and Information Science.

Deans of library schools were sent a letter inviting participation in this project. The deans asked interested faculty to incorporate this assignment into their teaching. The committee of judges received stories from more than 120 students. Students were asked to interview librarians to determine if, as a result of their work, they had had an impact on someone's life.

Through the students who participated, this assignment reached out to librarians in different parts of the country. The anecdotes that follow were judged to be the winners by the Right to Know Committee. These stories show librarians in different settings who work with a varying clientele. Congratulations to the faculty who incorporated this assignment into their courses, the students who gained insight into the nature of professional practice from their interviews with librarians, and the librarians themselves, who understood what it means to increase the right to know of the people who use the library.

Common Threads

As you read these stories, look for the common threads that run through them and other stories that show how librarians help people solve problems.

The first, and possibly the least obvious, is that these stories show how much the librarian in each case was trusted. When librarians become trusted information resources who are seen as being able to help people solve a problem, patrons then want to share stories about how

they were helped. Stories represent feedback that these librarians received about the nature of the service they provided—about how they helped someone learn something, find something, gain knowledge, or solve a problem. Without this kind of feedback, there are no stories about how librarians helped.

Second, there is a common concern for the people behind the questions. Librarians are well aware that they help people get through the maze of materials and resources. Librarians often speak in generalities. They know how to respond to different kinds of questions. These librarians know how they have helped a particular individual, a person. They helped as much by the approach they used as by the information they provided. When librarians know how they help individuals, they are better equipped to respond to questions in general, because they become aware of the impact of the interaction.

Finally, there is a sense of empowerment felt by the people whose lives were touched by librarians. That sense is accompanied by a show of gratitude and respect for the value of the work of these librarians.

The Stories

Student's Name: Leslie Horner Button
Library School: University of Rhode Island
Faculty Member: Professor Gale Eaton
Librarian: Michael Franceschi

Michael Franceschi, director of the Greenfield Public Library in Greenfield, Massachusetts, recognizes the important service the library provides to the town. "We have a very high level of usage by the community," Michael stated, "and we are very proud of the services we are able to provide." Michael regularly visits the local high school; the purpose of these excursions is part of a dual effort to inform the students of the information the library can provide and to encourage the students to consider librarianship as a profession as part of a "career day" at the school. This past autumn, Michael made such a visit to the Greenfield High School. A few weeks later, one of the students Michael addressed, Dan Beaubien, came to the library for assistance on a paper due for his history class; the topic was the Tet Offensive during the Vietnam War. Michael was working at the reference desk when Dan came in. Michael said that he showed him the available sources, which included a number of monographs, as well as a Time-Life series on the Vietnam War and other reference sources. "After I showed him the available material," Michael said, "I really did not think too much about our interaction until Dan returned approximately two weeks later to tell me that he had received an A on his paper. He said he got the A because of the assistance I provided," stated Michael.

"It is the 'every-person' concept that I believe is important in this profession," Michael admitted. Michael explained, "What I mean by this concept is it is the patron who comes in, who is ill equipped to handle the resources within the library, who may not know what questions to ask, yet who makes the effort to walk through that door and ask the questions, then builds upon what you have been able to show them." According to Michael, "This is the patron who makes everything worthwhile. It is a wonderful feeling to know that you have been able to really make a difference in that individual's life, no matter how small you think that contribution is." Michael concluded, "This is the true value of my being in the library profession, knowing I can enhance another individual's life because they are able to take the information I have shown them and do something positive with it."

Student's Name: Susan Shultz
Library School: Emporia State University
Faculty Member: Dr. John Agada
Librarian: Larry Busch

Larry Busch has worked in the Kansas City, Kansas, Public Library System for nearly twenty-five years. He is the type of reference librarian who knows his patrons' names; they enjoy this rapport and many ask for his service.

He remembers a recent incident. A Mr. Anderson called for information from the Kansas and Federal Statutes. He had been told by his social worker that the public library could provide details on legislation concerning Medicaid and Medicare. Mr. Anderson was totally disabled and asthmatic. He used a speaker phone so that he could communicate. Larry found relevant passages in the Kansas Statutes, and with the help of Jobeth Bradbury (head of the Wyandotte Library reference staff) was able to provide other information out of the 300s. Mr. Anderson was very thankful and wanted Larry's superior service documented. Because of Larry's intervention, Mr. Anderson discovered that he was indeed eligible for Medicaid benefits.

Larry adds, "If our life is never a success and we cannot say that we touched someone with our service then we will have failed—no matter how many statistical studies we do, no matter how many books we count, no matter how many films we are able to total up. If we have touched and interacted in a profound way, then we will be successful."

Student's Name: Elaine Donoghue
Library School: University of Rhode Island
Faculty Member: Professor Gale Eaton
Librarian: Janis Wolkenbreit

Janis Wolkenbreit, librarian at Crocker Farm Elementary School in Amherst, Massachusetts, was recently gratified to receive a letter from the mother of Johanna, one of her former students. Johanna moved to Pennsylvania at the end of the last school year and is now a seventh-grade student in her new junior high. She had lived in Amherst and attended Crocker Farm all of her school career. Her mother wrote to thank Janis for all that she had taught her daughter. Johanna is having a very difficult time in her new school because she is not adjusting and fitting in socially with the other students. The only things making her happy and helping her feel good about herself are the thinking and research skills that she learned from Janis and that have enabled her to excel in her schoolwork. Johanna's mother wrote that her "thinking and research skills are standing her in good stead and are what is keeping her going." Janis was touched that Johanna's mother would have taken the time to write this letter and, while sad for Johanna in her situation, was pleased that she was able to give her something to take with her.

Johanna's mother also sent a copy of her letter to the superintendent of schools. A letter like this could prove critical, because at a recent school committee meeting the superintendent proposed trimming the budget by eliminating all library aides at the four elementary schools in town. If approved, this proposal would take effect in the fall of 1992 and have a very negative effect on the library program at Crocker Farm. Janis feels that the first function of the library is to get the books out to the children and teachers. The library aides now handle all of the circulation, shelving, and other clerical tasks. If they are not there she will have to take the time away from teaching to perform those jobs. Perhaps if enough parents speak up, programs like this will be preserved, and other children will continue to have these valuable skills as they continue in their education.

Student's Name: Rose Ann Gubbins
Library School: State University of New York
**   at Buffalo**
Faculty Member: Professor Lorna Peterson
Librarian: Carol Bekar

Carol Bekar, librarian, established the Northern Studies Library at McGill University, Quebec, from 1976 to 1980. During this time, Hydro-Quebec, a provincial utility company, wanted to better utilize the vast water resources in northern Quebec to generate electricity. The most northern portions of the land in question were inhabited by the Inuit (Eskimo), a nomadic people with a fishing-and-hunting life-style. A lawsuit ensued.

Carol soon found that her library was a bevy of activity for people seeking information, for people using information, and for a meeting place for the Inuit and their legal counsel. The Northern Studies Library contained unique materials that could establish the land use and historical ownership of the land in question by the Inuit. Information included historical records of early explorers' expeditions, Canadian government reports by anthropologists for the Department of Indian Affairs, dissertations and theses, a reprint file of journal articles by subject area, and other journal literature. The collection, having material arranged by geographic area, was unique and very helpful to the Inuit's case.

In addition to materials in her own collection, Carol obtained land-use and land-reclamation materials from other libraries and also requested reports of Hydro-Quebec. Controversy resulted, as Hydro-Quebec considered these reports proprietary information, even though they contained critical information. All in all, Carol and her staff of five spent many hours providing information over the course of a year.

In interviewing Carol, I felt she learned a lot about native peoples, their culture, the dilemma of preserving culture versus making way for progress. The main benefit of Carol's efforts in this case was to give the Inuit the fairest settlement of money and land from the Quebec government. She also helped to preserve their way of life, and through the legal process and her own writings, more records were generated that could help other native cultures with similar issues.

Student's Name: Thomas G. Travers
Library School: University of Pittsburgh
Faculty Member: Dr. Sara Fine
Librarian: Joanne Howenstein

Joanne Howenstein, the librarian at Perrysville Elementary School in Pennsylvania, recalls an experience she had at the McIntyre Shelter, a temporary home for abused children who are wards of the court. She was reading stories to the children when one young boy with sad eyes got up from the floor to stand by her and stroke her neck. Mrs. Howenstein sat very still as he touched her, knowing how desperately this child needed to touch someone. She recalls her own emotion as she became aware that a simple story had reached this child and allowed him to reach out trustingly to a grown-up. She has never forgotten the power that a simple story can have in the life of a child.

Student's Name: Diane D. Eldridge
Library School: University of Pittsburgh
Faculty Member: Dr. Sara Fine
Librarian: Mary Vasilakis

Mary Vasilakis recalls the day in the early 1970s when she noticed a very high-level manager at the Nuclear Center fumbling through some general encyclopedias. Since he was obviously having difficulty finding what he was looking for in the highly specific collection of this special library, she asked, "What can I do to help you find what you need?" At these words, the manager turned to her with tears in his eyes and said, "My son has just been diagnosed with a rare form of leukemia, and I don't know what to do. I don't even know what it is." Mary said to him, "Let us help you find what you need. We'll use all our resources to find as much information for you as is available."

The library's reference staff began its search by contacting Falk Library of the Health Sciences at the University of Pittsburgh for books with background information on the topic. After supplying these, Mary asked her own manager for special permission to travel physically to Falk Library herself and spend the time and money necessary to get the needed information. At Falk Library, she discussed with the staff the possibility of using the newly available MEDLINE to check the journal literature for current research on leukemia and in particular this form of it. The MEDLINE files turned up some of the new protocols for treating the disease, giving the grieving father the ability to understand his son's illness to such an extent that he soon became the expert on the literature and was able to discuss cutting-edge therapy with his son's physicians, ensuring that the child had the advantage of the most current treatment available. His son survived the disease; and the technical library and its manager basked in the manager's gratitude and appreciation.

The field needs more stories. You can help. As you talk with your colleagues, take time to find out how they have helped someone. Think about your own experience. Remember those who came back to you after you helped them and told you how what you did helped. When people spontaneously tell you of their success and how information contributed to it, make a note and add the story to your file. As more librarians collect stories, they will become a new way of measuring the impact of library service—and your contribution to it—on people's lives.

Notes

1. Joan C. Durrance, "A Call to Action: The Power of Personal Stories," in *Your Right to Know: Librarians Make it Happen: Conference Within a Conference Background Papers*, ed. Elizabeth Curry (Chicago: American Library Assn., 1992).

2. Joan C. Durrance, *Serving Job Seekers and Career Changers: A Planning Manual for Public Libraries* (Chicago: American Library Assn., 1993).

Speaking Up
and Speaking Out

A United Voice in Washington
and Idaho—a Project in Progress

Mary M. Carr and Barbara C. Greever

This article chronicles the genesis and progress of Speaking Up and Speaking Out, a pilot project of the Washington Library Association (WLA), the Idaho Library Association (ILA), and the Idaho State Library. The project is funded by the World Book–American Library Association (ALA) Book Goal Awards, the participating state associations, the Idaho State Library, and Media Strategy, Inc. (MSI), Chicago.

The following abstract outlines the elements of the project:

Mary M. Carr, representative of the Washington Library Association, and Barbara C. Greever, representative of the Idaho Library Association, propose to develop a pilot media training package for use at the chapter level. With the contributed expertise of Susan L. Silk (MSI, Chicago), the authors will (1) assist Ms. Silk in the development and production of a training videotape, featuring Ms. Silk, to be used in conjunction with local resource persons who have "graduated" from Ms. Silk's American Library Association media training, (2) assist Ms. Silk in the development of training materials to be used in conjunction with the videotape, (3) develop evaluative instruments to be used to critique the training sessions, (4) hold twelve training sessions, six each in Washington and Idaho during the grant year, (5) develop a speakers' network in Idaho and Washington states, (6) develop recommendations regarding modification of this pilot

project prior to its use in the other ALA chapters, and (7) publish the results of this pilot project in *American Libraries* and media journals such as the *Gannett Center Journal*.

At the time of this writing the first two steps have been completed; between now and July 1993, the remainder will be accomplished.

From Idea to Award

This Washington-Idaho pilot project, like many others, started with an idea and a happy coincidence. During her two-year term as president of the Washington Library Association, Mary M. Carr gave considerable thought to librarians' seeming reluctance to speak out about issues vital to their profession. The Washington Library Association had learned to communicate effectively (at least to some extent) with state legislators, but rarely, if ever, did association representatives speak to the media or directly to groups of citizens. During her term as WLA president, she concluded that advocacy was essential if the profession was to survive, but she struggled to identify the appropriate mechanism needed to organize and train spokespersons. Her final presidential message to the WLA membership was "Go forth and advocate. Find ways to let others know your worth. The funding of our libraries and the education of tomorrow's librarians depend upon it." ("Hindsight," *Alki: The Washington Library Association Journal* 7, no.2 [July 1991], p.68)

Since Mary had expressed this sentiment repeatedly during her term, it is not surprising that Barbara Tolliver, the current president of WLA, appointed Mary as Washington's chapter representative to "The Right to Know— a United Voice: ALA Media Training and Speakers' Network." This day-long training session was held in San Antonio, January 24, 1992.

As circumstance would have it, Mary, who now works in northern Idaho, is also a current member of the Idaho Library Association Executive Board. At the fall board meeting, she asked Betty Holbrook, president of ILA, who would be appointed to represent Idaho. Barbara C. Greever, chair of the ILA Membership Committee, agreed to represent the Idaho chapter.

At the same meeting, Betty, in reviewing the ILA correspondence, mentioned that the American Library Association had sent the ILA a 1992 application form and guidelines for the World Book–ALA Goal Awards. She asked if any of the board members had an idea for a grant proposal.

Already Mary had begun to realize the difficulty of having only one representative from each chapter in the ALA Speakers' Network. One spokesperson cannot address all issues or be everywhere at once, especially in states such as Washington and Idaho, which cover large geographic areas. The network, if it is to be effective, has to grow to encompass people with varying library experiences dispersed throughout each state. This concern became the seed of an idea to expand the Speakers' Network. What better opportunity to expand this network than with grant funding? Mary took the application form and began to consider the possibilities.

The application form listed former grant recipients. From the list Mary learned that the speakers' training session that she and Barbara were about to attend had been funded in 1991 by this very grant. It seemed probable that ALA might be amenable to a proposal that would broaden the Speakers' Network. A cooperative venture, including two states, also seemed an intriguing notion. Hastily, a draft proposal was written before ALA Midwinter in San Antonio in order to provide a basis for discussion with members of the World Book– ALA Goal Awards Committee who were meeting during the conference. The original proposal suggested that Mary and Barbara be the media trainers for the two-state project.

On January 24, 1992, Mary and Barbara attended the day-long media training session featuring Susan L. Silk, founder and president of Media Strategy, Inc. The presentation was excellent but a bit overwhelming. That day

alone convinced both Mary and Barbara that media training should remain in the hands of the experts.

Armed with this realization, the next day they attended the World Book–ALA Goal Awards Committee meeting to present their proposal and ask the committee's advice. The committee, chaired by Phyllis Van Orden, was extremely receptive and helpful. It was intrigued with the notion that this would be a pilot project that could be replicated by other ALA chapters. The members urged Mary and Barbara to refine the proposal and suggested enlisting the services of a media specialist. The committee's suggestion confirmed what they already knew.

Since Ms. Silk had presented such an outstanding program only the day before, it seemed natural to approach her first. The opportunity presented itself that evening at a reception for Speakers' Network members hosted by ALA president Patricia Glass Schuman. Ms. Silk was not only receptive to the idea of extending the Speakers' Network, she agreed on the spot! It was determined that production of a training videotape would provide the flexibility needed to reach multiple audiences, at different times, in remote corners of both states.

Mary and Barbara's task was to finalize the proposal and submit it to the committee in March. This involved writing the rationale and outlining the project, as well as developing both calendar and budget. Ms. Silk reviewed the draft document, giving input particularly on the budget and the use of the videotape. It was fortunate that Barbara was scheduled to be in Chicago for a conference in February and was able to consult with Ms. Silk personally.

It was envisioned that the videotape presentation would be presented in six locations in each state within the grant year. This would involve nearly fourteen thousand miles of travel for the facilitators, Mary and Barbara. Travel costs, combined with the cost of producing the videotape and accompanying training materials, yielded a $30,600 budget, with $19,100 in actual expenditures and $11,500 in in-kind contributions donated by MSI. Matching funds were needed, since the most that could be requested from the committee was $10,000. Mary and Barbara approached their respective state associations, as well as the Idaho State Library, for funding. The associations and the ISL were generous in their support, contributing a total of $9,100 to the project.

Mary and Barbara also solicited letters of support from the contributors, as well as Gloria Leonard (ALA Special Presidential Right to Know Committee, Seattle Public Library) and ALA president Patricia Glass Schuman. Gloria expressed her excitement about "the potential of having this pilot project in the region." She concluded that "Washington and Idaho can effectively team up to provide a national model." President Schuman stated that this project would "truly show that librarians do—indeed—make it happen!" The proposal was submitted.

Several months of waiting followed. In May the committee sent official notification that the Washington and Idaho Library Associations had received the award. The committee had granted the two chapters the entire $10,000 as one award, instead of the usual two $5,000 awards given to two ALA units.

The Project

No sooner had the letter arrived than Mary and Barbara contacted Ms. Silk. Work on the videotape script began immediately. Within a matter of weeks, Ms. Silk and the staff at MSI wrote a rough draft, which was sent to Mary and Barbara by telefacsimile. As a result of their input, as well as comments from members of both chapters, the draft went through several iterations. Significant progress was made quickly, thus allowing Ms. Silk, Mary, and Barbara to finalize the script while attending the ALA annual conference in San Francisco, June 25 to July 2, 1992.

The annual conference was capped by the inaugural banquet, which took place on the evening of July 1. Part of the inaugural festivities was the presentation of the ALA–World Book Goal Award. The presentation was made by President Schuman and Joan S. Sain (World Book Educational Products). Mary and Barbara happily accepted the award on behalf of their associations. The $10,000 check was welcome because the project was already underway.

In mid-July Mary and Barbara traveled to Chicago to assist in the shooting and editing of the video. The experience proved to be an educational one. Like many of MSI's clients, Mary and Barbara had no idea how much work was required to produce a videotape. They had been told that the schedule was to shoot on Tuesday and edit on Saturday. What they failed to understand was that there were many intervening steps that were time and labor intensive. (So much for a trip to the Art Institute, or even Marshall Field's!) Mary and Barbara spent nearly ninety hours, and MSI staff contributed well over two hundred hours during the five days of production. Mary and Barbara left on Sunday with the videotape nearly finished. In August minor changes were made to the videotape, and the accompanying training guide was completed.

The videotape and guide are divided into two main sections: "Effective Public Speaking" and "Effective Media Relations." The training materials provide "basic and time-tested tips to sharpen existing [public speaking] skills and introduce spokespersons to the mass media."

The training sessions are designed to make participants "media savvy," to quote Ms. Silk. She defines "media savvy" as "creating a level playing field, knowing where the media are coming from, so that you can more effectively gain media attention."

While in Chicago a contract with MSI, which specifies the use that can be made of the media training package, was negotiated. Use is limited to Washington and Idaho for the duration of the pilot project. It was also decided that the training package's premiere would be in September during two focus groups, one scheduled to be held in Boise, Idaho, the other slated for Seabeck, Washington.

The focus groups will be composed primarily of members of the two state association boards. Ms. Silk will also attend the presentations to the focus groups. The purpose for the focus groups is twofold: (1) to refine the presentation techniques and review the training materials and (2) to increase the associations' support for the project. Support will be critical to ensure participation in the training sessions and, more important, to develop and maintain the Speakers' Network in both Washington and Idaho.

This pilot project has become an integral part of WLA's public relations plan, which is presently under development. In Idaho it is hoped that the project will provide the impetus for ILA to determine its priorities for public relations throughout the state.

At the time of this writing, the focus-group sessions have yet to take place. Furthermore, the twelve presentations are just being scheduled, some for fall 1992, others for spring 1993. Mary and Barbara will evaluate the presentations using an instrument based on the one developed by MSI and used at the media training session in San Antonio.

Mary and Barbara, on behalf of their respective associations, will ask media training participants to commit to making two media contacts in the first year following the training and three contacts in the second year. The participants will receive forms on which they can report their experiences. These reports will be used to measure the strength and continued viability of the Speakers' Network in Washington and Idaho. In effect, these instruments will be the ultimate means of evaluating the success of the pilot project.

Conclusion

As the grant year progresses, more and more members of WLA and ILA will acquire and refine the skills necessary to communicate effectively with the media and with the public. As a result, important issues facing the library community will begin to receive the increased attention that they deserve. To quote Ms. Silk, "Should this project prove successful—should well-trained and willing local librarians be effective in their efforts to speak up and speak out to the public about those issues facing librarians and libraries in America today—it is possible that this project will be spread across the country to enable librarians everywhere to join in the struggle for recognition and support of the important work they are doing."

Watch for a report during summer or fall 1993 detailing the outcomes of this pilot project.

How Your Right to Know Took Root in Rochester,

or

Viburnum are a-Bloomin' in New York State!

Amy Small

When the American Library Association president Patricia Glass Schuman selected "Your Right to Know: Librarians Make It Happen" as her presidential theme for 1991–92, little did she know that the essence of this theme would be taken up by the New York Library Association (NYLA), not only in 1991 and 1992 but in 1993, 1994, and 1995. In August 1992 the Viburnum Foundation of Rochester awarded the New York Library Association a three-year $335,000 grant for a public-awareness and marketing plan to improve awareness and support for libraries. The following is the story of how this all came about.

Background

Janet Welch, NYLA president and director of the Rochester Regional Library Council, announced the primary goal for her 1992 presidential term is to implement the recommendations of the 1990 Governor's Conference and the 1991 White House Conference on Library and Information Services. Citizen delegates and public officials at the 1990 New York Governor's Conference identified library public relations as a weak point and strongly urged a comprehensive and aggressive public relations program. Conference delegates emphasized that "library services are indispensable to the development of human potential, the advancement of civilization, and the strengthening of enlightened self-government." However, delegates selected from the general public and library supporters also expressed a particularly strong belief that more needs to be done to inform the public about the rich mixture of services available to them in their libraries.

In February 1992 a small family foundation in New York, the Viburnum Foundation of Rochester, expressed interest in funding a program to increase the public's knowledge of libraries and to create a better understanding of the importance of library and information services. The Viburnum Foundation has helped to support the development of "Check-It Out," a daily radio program on libraries that is broadcast on public radio stations. Harold Hacker, the director emeritus of the Rochester Public Library, the Monroe County Library System, and a delegate to the Governor's Conference, provided a valuable connection between the foundation and NYLA, serving as the foundation's representative to NYLA. Subsequently, Viburnum offered NYLA a $10,000 planning grant to develop a three-year program to increase support for libraries. The grant for each of the three years was projected at $100,000.

In March 1992 NYLA accepted the planning grant and reactivated the Public Awareness Committee to develop, implement, and monitor the proposed statewide public relations plan. The committee members included librarians, library trustees, Friends, and public relations professionals who represent school, public, academic, and special libraries. The president of ALA, Patricia Glass Schuman, joined the seventeen-member committee and was a key participant in the subcommittee that drafted the final proposal. Peggy Barber, ALA communications director, attended the June meeting and also offered her support. Every effort will be made to continue this advocacy after the grant project is completed.

In August 1992 the Viburnum Foundation board of directors awarded $135,000 to NYLA for the first year of the three-year project. Funding for the next two years is expected to be $100,000 each year.

The ALA Connection

The NYLA program includes careful coordination with existing public relations and marketing efforts, principally "Your Right to Know: Librarians Make It Happen." This ALA theme built on the collective strength of the ALA and the state chapters to tell the library story to the media forcefully and effectively. It was also easily adaptable for academic, public, school, and special librarians.

The ALA campaign emphasized training, as will the NYLA project. It will be a priority to educate and train librarians, trustees, and library advocates to promote effective public relations and marketing at the local level. Every effort will be made to continue this advocacy after the grant project is completed.

> The ALA campaign included active participation through media training for a network of library spokespersons. Similar activities will be incorporated into the New York plan, which hopes to develop a grass-roots network of five hundred trained library advocates.

The NYLA campaign will build on all the ALA activities, including innovative programs such as the Call for America's Libraries. The New York project will utilize similar methods to provide initiatives and opportunities to deliver the library message. The NYLA campaign will plan unified statewide print and electronic-media coverage.

The New York Connection

There is already a precedent in New York State for cooperation with ALA initiatives. Susan Keitel, executive director of NYLA, shared the ALA media training she received (in January 1992) by (1) doing radio interviews and providing opportunities for Janet Welch to do interviews; (2) incorporating many of the right-to-know ideas into the Viburnum proposal; (3) sending letters to all 211 New York State legislators explaining the Your Right to Know and Call for America's Libraries campaigns; (4) disseminating information to the NYLA infrastructure through NYLINE, which reaches hundreds of sites statewide. Every effort will be made to continue this advocacy after the grant project is completed.

Even before the Right to Know campaign, New York State and NYLA effectively adapted some ALA ideas. A striking example is the Night of 1000 Stars/Great American Read Aloud, which ALA initiated in 1990. This event, held during National Library Week, is a celebration of libraries and reading. Celebrities and special guests come to the library to read aloud from their favorite books. The event was repeated by ALA with great success in 1991 and 1992. In New York State the Night of 1000 Stars became the Night of 7000 Stars for the state's seven thousand libraries. Audiences estimated at four hundred thousand participated statewide. It was a cooperative project sponsored by the New York Library Association, the New York State Association of Library Boards, the New York State Education Department, the New York State Library, and Imagination Celebration. Every effort will be made to continue this advocacy after the grant project is completed.

Conclusion

The Governors' Conference and the White House Conference were mandates for libraries to market themselves more effectively. For the last several years a ground swell of support for libraries has been building. The ALA campaign Your Right to Know: Librarians Make It Happen was an outstanding example of how to build on this support. The initiatives and results of that campaign provide a powerful precedent. The Viburnum Foundation of Rochester will enable the New York Library Association to further the goals and objectives of the ALA campaign and to expand them so that public, school, academic, and special libraries in rural, suburban, and urban communities in New York State can fulfill their mission.

The New York Library Association believes that the momentum from Your Right to Know, which led, in part, to the Viburnum Foundation of Rochester grant, will substantially contribute to increased awareness of the need for ongoing library marketing and public relations efforts.

Message

What Libraries Can Do for You; What You Can Do for Libraries; or What Libraries Need in Order to Maintain, Improve, and Expand Services.

Goals

1. Inform potential users about the wide variety of services and materials available to them from library systems and member libraries.
2. Create a better understanding on the part of government officials, other decision makers, and the general public of the significance of libraries and librarians and how they relate to people of all ages in all walks of life.
3. Promote books, reading, and literacy in people's lives, especially in the lives of children.
4. Improve library funding so that libraries will be better able to achieve the goals adopted at the 1990 New York Governor's Conference on Library and Information Services.
5. Focus attention on the contributions libraries make in the field of education, especially for people in rural and urban areas where library funding is inadequate.

6. Serve as a model public relations and marketing program that can be replicated nationally.

Methods

1. Work with a public relations firm and other communications professionals to create and implement an imaginative, aggressive statewide public relations campaign.
2. Create and adapt special events and initiatives to focus attention on libraries, books, reading, literacy, and the need for support.
3. Develop a program to train librarians and other library supporters to be effective advocates for libraries and to build a broad, deep, and committed constituency and keep it active.
4. Develop partnerships with organizations in the community, including public-private partnerships, and strengthen relationships among Friends, trustees, and other advocates as they come together to promote, propagate, promulgate, and publicize libraries, literacy, and learning.

Public Relations Campaign Plan

Texas Library Association

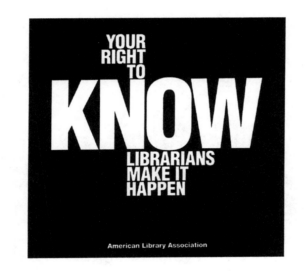

Texas Library Association
Public Relations Presentation

Situation: The Texas Library Association has issued a proposal for a public relations campaign for libraries and librarians in Texas. Funding available for the one-year campaign is $26,900.

Campaign Goals: The Texas Library Association has modified its original proposal to concentrate solely on improving the image of librarians and of libraries.

Suggested Campaign Strategy

Target Audience: 18-49. Young adults and young parents will have the greatest impact on libraries. They will not only be users but will also be instigators of library use by others. They are also the ones who vote on library bonds and the ones who are active in community activities.

The general public needs to be made aware of the intelligent and resourceful people who make libraries work—the librarians!

Campaign Theme/Slogan

The campaign theme would be chosen by TLA during the initial research and formulation of the public relations plan. Our working themes which may be changed at a later date are "Get the Facts: Ask a Librarian," or "Be in the Know: Ask a Librarian." These are powerful messages that play on our society's need for information.

The emotional impact of the library should not be underrated. While the library provides many physical services (books, compact discs, videocassettes, films, computers, typewriters, library staff knowledge, public meeting rooms, etc.), the library also provides a cultural exchange for people. Libraries have a social as well as an informational role.

Strategy

The Texas Library Association is an organization of more than 5,000 members, comprising public, school, academic, corporate, and special collection libraries. As we are a society rich in information, libraries can play a vital role in productive, successful lives. Libraries provide us with information that we would spend hours compiling on our own. The specific knowledge of "where to look for what" is part of what makes librarians an invaluable resource in our information-based culture.

Because of the narrowed focus of this project, we have modified the public relations strategies to include a basic core program with additional public relations ideas. We believe that the strategies presented would be the best use of available time and resources.

Core Public Relations Plan

1. Public Relations Plan
2. Electronic Feature Stories
3. Media Placements
4. TV Magazine Placements
5. Ads/buttons
6. Radio Public Service Announcements
   Additional Public Relations Items
7. Library Block Parties
8. Post/Pre Evaluation
9. TV ID Tag (PSA)

Public Relations Strategy

Public Relations Plan: DeLaune and Associates believes in a thorough understanding of our clients' businesses. In order to better focus the public's attention on the diversity of Texas libraries, one of the first steps in the campaign would be a compilation of libraries throughout the state based on their public relations potential. Documents such as the *Directory of Special Libraries and Information Centers in Texas* would be used in preparing this compilation. The Texas State Library in Austin would be invaluable for our research, as would individual members of the TLA staff and TLA Public Information Committee.

We would also create a written timeline in a more structured form to follow based on this extensive research and the items chosen by TLA on which to concentrate.

Electronic Feature Stories: TLA would target eight major markets in Texas. We have identified the markets as follows: Austin, Dallas, Houston, San Antonio, Corpus Christi, McAllen, Fort Worth, and Lubbock. These areas also have television and radio stations which reach into smaller regional cities and towns. By broadly covering these areas, we will reach as much of Texas as possible, including all geographical and ethnic populations.

Much of the library coverage would be timed to coincide with National Literacy Month in September, National Library Week (April 14-20), and National Children's Book Week in November. Again, all public relations work would be more narrowly focused after detailed evaluation of the Texas Library Associations target markets.

Media Placements: DeLaune and Associates would write and place feature stories in area magazines about interesting librarians and library collections. These stories might involve famous Texans who have used the library in their particular accomplishments, interesting or unusual collections at Texas libraries, and interesting librarians. From screening the newspapers in Texas over the past two months, we have discovered that Texas libraries are already getting a lot of print coverage. (Please see back page.)

Since Texas libraries are already getting coverage in newspapers, TLA may want to concentrate solely on magazine stories (*D Magazine, Austin Magazine, Houston Metropolitan*). To reach a large segment of the adult target market, we would concentrate on regional and airline general interest magazines.

Some examples are:

American Airlines *American Way* magazine
Houston Public Library Central Collection
"Rare Religious Manuscripts on Display"

Continental magazine
University of Texas at Austin
Eugene C. Barker
Texas History Center
"Tracing Austin's History"

Southwest Airlines *Spirit* magazine
Marion Koogler
McNay Art Museum Library
"Art Students Execute Pencil Renderings of Art
    Collection Works Based on Museum Originals"

Texas Monthly
"Five Fascinating Texas Librarians"

TV Magazine Placements: These shows are the talk shows, and morning and evening news shows which are not the hard newscasts but the more entertaining news shows focusing on lifestyle and cultural issues. Again, we would garner attention in the target markets with a focus on an interesting librarian or library collection.
Ads/Buttons: DeLaune and Associates would produce a series of promotional items (see examples) centered around the theme of the campaign. The small, one-column ad could be revised into a bookmark to be handed out at each library location. Each librarian across the state in all the various libraries from public to school to special collection would wear the buttons to encourage patrons to view their librarian as the information-rich source he or she is.
Radio Public Service Announcements: We would create a series of 60 second radio PSAs which highlight TLA's campaign theme. Since literacy is a concern of many radio stations in their public service goals, many stations would be open to running a PSA which focuses on Texas libraries and librarians. The spots would feature Texas authors or public figures.

Additional PublicRelations Strategies

Library Block Parties: During the summer of 1991, Texas Library Association would sponsor two Library Block Parties in two major markets in Texas. We would feature book signings by famous Texas authors. (Larry McMurtry, Liz Carpenter, Kinky Friedman, Whitley Streiber) We would also consider finding a local radio or television station in each block party's city to cosponsor the event. This would help publicize the event and purchase the valuable advertising space.

TLA and DeLaune and Associates would set an expected attendance goal and use that goal as a form of evaluation. Public relations stories in both print and electronic media would get the public excited about coming out to the library for this event. Special events are also great internal energizers as everyone working in the library will be enthusiastic about the party.

Refreshments and decorations would add to the festive atmosphere emphasizing the entertainment value libraries can offer their patrons.

Pre/Post Evaluation: An in-house questionnaire of 400 library patrons would be done in four locations at the beginning of the campaign and at a set date later in the campaign. While the campaign is for a one-year period, image change takes years as we must alter the way people think about certain situations. A definite change will be shown from the pre and post tests although the ideas set forth in this campaign should be continued for a two to five year period to have a lasting impact.

After the inauguration of the campaign, we would monitor press mentions monthly to determine the dollar volume of the public relations coverage which we were receiving. This figure would reflect the amount of money which it would have cost to purchase the space as advertising. Based on the final budget set for public relations by TLA, a goal would be set for the dollar value of the public relations.

TV ID Tag (PSA): DeLaune and Associates would produce a 10 second animated television identification tag. This short colorful spot would feature the TLA theme with a catchy phrase.

Corporate Sponsorship

Since TLA has set some major goals for their campaign, it may be advisable to seek corporate sponsorships to help fund more of the possible activities. We have made an initial contact with BOOKSTOP, for whom we have done public relations work in Texas and in Florida, about the possibility of their interest in such a project.

Since BOOKSTOP began as a Texas-based corporation, we believe that there could be a natural connection between that corporation and this project. BOOKSTOP currently has stores in five Texas cities, and they have indicated that they would be interested in receiving a proposal for involvement in campaigns in those cities. In addition, we would suggest approaching other Texas-based corporations as well as Texas-based foundations which have a particular interest in literacy.

Creative Team

Account Executive: Sara Rider
Public Relations Coordinator: Amy Smith
Graphic Designer: Joe Medrano
Public Relations Assistant: Kay Morris

Texas Library Association
Public Relations Presentation Budget

Core Public Relations Plan

1. Public Relations Plan $ 1,775
2. Electronic Feature Stories (8 cities) $ 1,450
3. Media Placements (6 magazines) $ 2,730
4. TV Magazine Placements (6 shows) $ 1,705
5. Ads/buttons Design $ 2,000
6. Radio PSA (:60 seconds) $ 4,500
    Subtotal $14,160

Additional Public Relations Strategies

7. Library Block Parties (2 cities)
    Includes Ad design for parties** $ 7,400
8. Post/Pre Evaluation $ 5,597
9. TV ID Tag (10 second) $ 8,000

**Assuming radio or TV cosponsorship of the block parties or a possible corporate sponsorship who would be responsible for buying media space to advertise the block parties.

Budgets do not include the cost of copies, deliveries, sales tax, long distance, travel, or printing unless otherwise indicated. Final charges may vary by 10 percent. Charges in excess of 10 percent require a change order. All contracts are performable in Austin, Travis county.

Press Clips

Oct. - Nov. 1990

Houston	11
San Antonio	16
Austin	16
Dallas	21
Ft. Worth	7
McAllen	3
Lubbock	7
Corpus Christi	3
Total clips in all Texas newspapers	1,193

Bad Times Need Good Libraries

Massachusetts Library Association

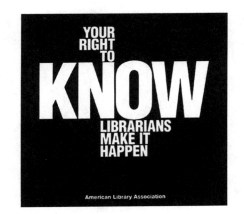

MASSACHUSETTS
LIBRARY
ASSOCIATION

TO: PUBLIC LIBRARY DIRECTORS OF MASSACHUSETTS
FR: THE PUBLIC RELATIONS COMMITTEE OF MLA
      (Ellen Rainville, Chair, 508-692-5557)
RE: DESK FLYER, PROCLAMATION AND NEWS RELEASE SERIES....
      "BAD TIMES NEED GOOD LIBRARIES"
DT: 3/13/92

Please find enclosed the following Public Relations
Materials for your use during the current budget season and as
promotionals for National Library Week, April 5 - 11, 1992:

    1) 1 "BAD TIMES NEED GOOD LIBRARIES" Camera-Ready DESK FLYER

    2) 15 Camera-ready Press Releases (Theme: "If you're finding
the cost of modern life slightly unaffordable, you can't afford
not to check out your Public Library!"). You may wish to number
these by hand and use all or some of them sequentially...submit
them to your local paper, read them as radio spots, enlarge them
as posters, etc., etc.

    3) Proclamation for your City Council, Board of Selectmen,
Town Manager, or Mayor, etc. saluting your Library and
recognizing National Library Week

    Please let the Public Relations Committee know how these
items worked for you, or didn't work....by calling the Chair (see
above).

    We also strongly urge your participation in the ALA Radio
Rally and Call for America's Libraries Campaign. By calling 1 -
800-530-8888, your patrons will help create a nation-wide
grassroots lobbying list on behalf of all libraries. You should
have received information on this Right-to-Know Campaign through
the Regional delivery system.

    We hope this PR campaign works for your library, and that we
have sent you something that saves you time and effort, while
still promoting services you offer. Let us know how it goes, and
best of luck!

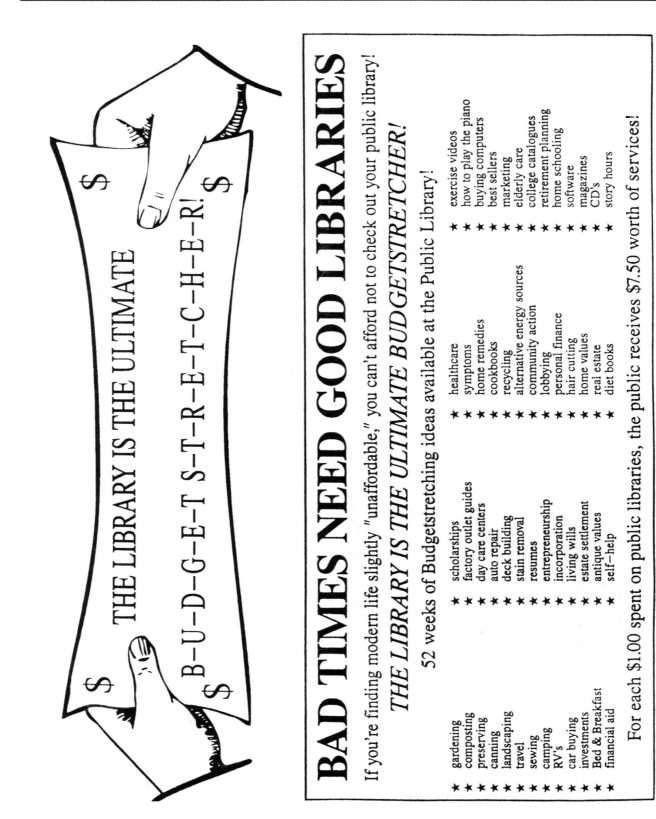

THE LIBRARY IS THE ULTIMATE

B–U–D–G–E–T S–T–R–E–T–C–H–E–R!

BAD TIMES NEED GOOD LIBRARIES

If you're finding modern life slightly "unaffordable," you can't afford not to check out your public library!

THE LIBRARY IS THE ULTIMATE BUDGETSTRETCHER!

52 weeks of Budgetstretching ideas available at the Public Library!

- ★ gardening
- ★ composting
- ★ preserving
- ★ canning
- ★ landscaping
- ★ travel
- ★ sewing
- ★ camping
- ★ RV's
- ★ car buying
- ★ investments
- ★ Bed & Breakfast
- ★ financial aid

- ★ scholarships
- ★ factory outlet guides
- ★ day care centers
- ★ auto repair
- ★ deck building
- ★ stain removal
- ★ resumes
- ★ entrepreneurship
- ★ incorporation
- ★ living wills
- ★ estate settlement
- ★ antique values
- ★ self—help

- ★ healthcare
- ★ symptoms
- ★ home remedies
- ★ cookbooks
- ★ recycling
- ★ alternative energy sources
- ★ community action
- ★ lobbying
- ★ personal finance
- ★ hair cutting
- ★ home values
- ★ real estate
- ★ diet books

- ★ exercise videos
- ★ how to play the piano
- ★ buying computers
- ★ best sellers
- ★ marketing
- ★ elderly care
- ★ college catalogues
- ★ retirement planning
- ★ home schooling
- ★ software
- ★ magazines
- ★ CD's
- ★ story hours

For each $1.00 spent on public libraries, the public receives $7.50 worth of services!

Budget Stretcher #1:

Mary McCorkle is planning a nifty weekend in Paris this April -- thanks to her Public Library!

Her salary as a secretary made a tax accountant's fee a little beyond her reach. So Mary stopped off at the public library on the way home from work, picked up some tax forms, and came across a whole shelf full of self-help books. She took a few of them home and studied them, intelligent woman that she is, and found enough deductions - all legal, of course - to fund that terrific airfare she saw advertised in Sunday's paper. Mary doesn't waste time, that's for sure. And she knows how to use her library's resources. Here are some of the books the public library offered:

Official IRS Tax Guide
J.K. Lasser's Your Income Tax
Guide to Income Tax Preparation
Official MASSTAX Guide

Visit your Public Library -- who knows where it will take you!

If you're finding the cost of modern life slightly unaffordable,
you can't afford not to check out your public library!

Budget Stretcher # :

Sam Singleton wheeled a deal -- thanks to the Public Library!

Sam Singleton was in the market for a new car, but almost "blew a gasket" over the latest sticker prices! Before he walked into another showroom, he wanted to know the comparative costs and care ratings on the new models, *and* the value of his old car...Sam cruised over to the public library to consult *Consumer Reports* magazine on new features and prices of the latest domestic and foreign models. The library also had other car guides, such as *Motor Trends* magazine, the *EPA Fuel Economy Estimates Gas Mileage Guide*, and the *Complete Car Cost Guide.*

Knowing he would be making one of the "three most expensive" purchases of a lifetime, Sam wanted the best trade-in value for his old car and the certain knowledge that he would move from behind the steering wheel of a gas guzzler to a new economy model.

Visit your Public Library -- for a real driver's education!

If you're finding the cost of modern life slightly unaffordable,
you can't afford not to check out your public library!

Budget Stretcher # :

Liz Fulton is a garbage collector -- thanks to her Public Library!

Black banana peels, slimy lettuce, rotten potatoes - all are treasures for
Liz. You see, for years, Liz had been a February gardener. When the
seed and bulb catalogs arrived in mid-winter, she would dream of her
summer flower beds, her fall vegetable harvest, and the money she could
save all year by making creative gifts from her gardens. Yet when the
planting season arrived, Liz would find her garden soil too sandy, dry,
rocky and alkaline. Then one day at the library she discovered a book
revealing the glories of garbage. Composting would solve her gardening
problems, help save the environment, and save Liz some money to boot.
Liz's sister helped by building a compost bin with directions she found in
a magazine borrowed from the library. Now Liz has rich, thick, compost
full of growing nutrients and a garden which equals her February dreams.
Here are some of the materials the public library offered:

> *Let it Rot! The Gardeners' Guide to Composting*
> *Garbage As You Like It*
> *Rodale Guide to Composting*
> *A Garden for All Seasons*
> *Organic Homes and Gardens Magazine*

Visit your Public Library -- a great value that's dirt cheap!

*If you're finding the cost of modern life slightly unaffordable,
you can't afford not to check out your public library!*

Budget Stretcher #2:

Mike Columbo's dog doesn't scratch anymore -- thanks to his Public Library!

See, Mike doesn't like to use aerosol sprays or poisonous pesticides on his retriever. He figures it's bad for the ozone layer and the environment and very expensive, to boot. It can't be doing the dog's health much good either. Mike really cares about having a safe and healthy environment for his family to grow up in - but that scratching was really driving him crazy! He found some books in the library that told him how to use some common, non-toxic substances, like orange rind, to ease Samson's (the dog) itches. Mike's wife Lucy was happy, too. She was able to cut a few dollars off the weekly shopping budget by finding simple, effective and environmentally safe household cleaning solutions that she could concoct in her own kitchen. Here are some of the books the library offered:

Earthright: What You Can Do in Your Home and Community to Save Our Environment

The Green Lifestyle Handbook: (1001 Ways You Can Heal the Earth)

50 Simple Things Kids Can Do to Save the Earth

Home Ecology: Simple and Practical Ways to Green Your Home

Clean & Green: The Complete Guide to Non-toxic and Environmentally Safe Housekeeping

Visit your public library - Save the planet *and* some scratch!

If you're finding the cost of modern life slightly unaffordable, you can't afford not to check out your public library!

Budget Stretcher # :

Mary Jane Jackson got a ticket to a "free" vacation -- thanks to her Public Library!

Knowing that a trip was impossible during school vacation week, what with her concerns about her husband's job, Mary Jane used her library card to get a "free" vacation with the kids. Tuesday was the library's Drop-In Story Hour, Wednesday was Movie Day at the library, and Thursday she picked up the library's free pass to the Children's Museum. The children's librarian even came up with a book on car games for the youngsters! Friday Mary Jane made it through the supper preparations by putting on the library's video of "The Little Mermaid." Of course, vacation week ended with the kids' favorite pastime -- snuggling together and sharing bedtime stories from the library's children's collection.

Visit your Public Library -- for a moneyless vacation!

If you're finding the cost of modern life slightly unaffordable, you can't afford not to check out your public library!

Budget Stretcher # :

Joe Godfrey got his "dream" vacation without the "nightmare" prices -- thanks to the Public Library!

Joe Godfrey planned his "dream" family vacation to Walt Disney World, but got there at "bargain prices!" Making the first stop on his trip the local public library, Joe found sources to plot the best routes, the most affordable campgrounds, the best Bed & Breakfast stops, and the lowest hotel rates to the "most popular man-made attraction on the planet" -- Walt Disney World. Joe got everything he wanted -- a warm climate, water sports, lot of activities for the kids, reasonable rates and good restaurants -- a "dream" vacation without the "nightmare" prices!

Visit your Public Library -- and earn your "mouse ears!"

If you're finding the cost of modern life slightly unaffordable, you can't afford not to check out your public library!

Budget Stretcher # :

Phil Young can barbecue once again . . . thanks to his Public Library!

Phil's favorite way of cooking on hot summer nights was literally ripped away from him when his old patio collapsed during a fierce wind storm. Handy person that he is, Phil headed for his public library and checked out some books and videos on designing and building porches and decks. Armed with this information and a small settlement from his home-owner's policy he built a screened-in porch with a deck on either side. Now Phil can really cook! With the money he saved by doing the work himself he purchased some comfortable outdoor furniture so he can sit back and enjoy the fruits of his labors. Some of the books available at the public library were:

> *Time Life Books - Porches and Patios*
> *Better Homes and Gardens Deck and Patio Projects You Can Build*
> *Sunset Patio Book*
> *Family Handyman Magazine*
> *Home Mechanix*

Visit your Public Library -- something to build your future on!

If you're finding the cost of modern life slightly unaffordable,
you can't afford not to check out your public library!

Budget Stretcher # :

John Smith went to work today -- thanks to his Public Library!

Sounds ordinary, but after several months out of work John thinks driving to his new job is wonderful. And on his way home he's returning the last of the books he got from his public library that helped him get that job. John made good use of the career guides, resume and cover letter handbooks, company directories, and job banks. And with the library's selection of newspapers and journals, he had access to a wealth of job listings.

John knew he didn't necessarily need a headhunter - he just needed to use his head!

Visit your Public Library -- the place to go to get ahead!

*If you're finding the cost of modern life slightly unaffordable,
you can't afford not to check out your public library!*

Budget Stretcher # :

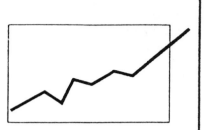

The members of the Board reached a "mutual" agreement -- thanks to the Public Library!

Joan Walker knew nothing about mutual funds, but with a little help from her public library she was able to make a solid recommendation to the Board on where they should invest their trust funds. Using information she got from the library books on investment services, business magazines, and financial newspapers, Joan was able to put together a presentation for the Board that was "mutually satisfying." And now that the Board has made its decision, Joan will be going back to the library to keep them informed on how their fund is performing.

When every dollar counts, isn't it nice to feel good about what you've done with yours?

Visit your Public Library -- where your investment pays off!

If you're finding the cost of modern life slightly unaffordable, you can't afford not to check out your public library!

Budget Stretcher # :

Little Miss Muffet no longer eats "curds and whey" -- thanks to her Public Library!

Little Miss Muffet sat on her tuffet
Sick of her curds and whey,
The spider beside her, gladly advised her,
To Visit Her Library Today!

After a lifetime of eating "curds and whey," Miss Muffet could not believe the array of cookbooks, new recipes, ethnic cooking tips, and nutritional and vitamin information available at the public library! The public library was "stuffed" with classic favorites: Peas Porridge Hot, Peas Porridge Cold, Hot Cross Buns, Gingerbread men, Plum Pudding, Blackbird pie, and of course, that favorite . . . *tofuburgers!*

Don't know what to cook tonight? (Don't know what "curds and whey" are?) Get into a new rhyme and rhythm at the public library.

Visit your Public Library -- for a new "whey" of cooking!

If you're finding the cost of modern life slightly unaffordable, you can't afford not to check out your public library!

Budget Stretcher # :

Joe can now sit back and relax -- thanks to his Public Library!

Joe had become a worrier. He worried about everything - his job, his children, his puppy, his health, and finances. He worried that he worried too much. His doctor told him he worried too much. Then one day, while Joe was waiting for his son at the library, he began browsing through the stacks of books. He discovered books on relaxation techniques and relieving stress through exercise and healthy diets. He sat down to read in a quiet, peaceful area of the library. In fact, Joe began to enjoy himself. He even forgot to worry -- he almost forgot his son who found him an hour and a half later, reading and relaxing at his public library.

Some of the materials the library had available to help Joe relax were:

Harvard Medical School Health Letter
Harvard Medical School Mental Health Letter
Prevention Magazine
Mount Sinai School of Medicine Complete Book of Nutrition
Complete Guide to Symptoms, Illness and Surgery

Visit your Public Library -- the therapeutic, low-cost alternative.

*If you're finding the cost of modern life slightly unaffordable,
you can't afford not to check out your public library!*

Budget Stretcher # :

Dana Davis found a whole new world . . . at the Public Library!

Before learning about a free literacy program at his local library, letters were just a jumble and job applications were something to be avoided. At 36, Dana was tired of bluffing his way through situations that required reading. He found that by working with his trained tutor two nights a week for a year, reading went from being a chore to something he could finally get a handle on. As letters and words became part of his life, Dana felt better about himself, especially around neighborhood parents and the guys at work. Now he can get better jobs, read with his kids and discover whole new worlds . . . at his public library. Thanks to volunteers, literacy programs and caring librarians, learning to read was free.

Visit your Public Library -- it's never too late to learn to read !

If you're finding the cost of modern life slightly unaffordable, you can't afford not to check out your public library!

Budget Stretcher # :

Madeline Washington earns a higher education at a lower cost -- thanks to her Public Library!

With the downturn in the economy Madeline, like a lot of other people, was laid off from her job. Not one to be defeated, Madeline visited her public library. Reading some books in the library's education section convinced her to follow her dream and return to school. Her friends asked how she would ever pay for tuition without a regular job, but Madeline already had an answer for them. She had found enough information in the books at her public library to show her how to seek out and obtain financial aid through work-study programs at a nearby university. Here are some of the books the public library offered:

> *Barron's Profiles of American Colleges*
> *Peterson's College Guide*
> *The Gourman Report - A Rating of Graduate and Professional Programs*
> *College Blue Books*

Visit your Public Library -- continuing education for life !

If you're finding the cost of modern life slightly unaffordable, you can't afford not to check out your public library!

Budget Stretcher # :

Robin Robinson got her money back with interest! -- thanks to her Public Library!

Robin recently changed jobs and was going to have to leave her apartment in a triple-decker. She didn't have a lease and vaguely remembered something about "tenant at will." After talking to a friend who had called a library for landlord/tenant information, Robin decided to drop by the library on her way home from work. The librarian showed her how to use the Massachusetts General Laws and handbooks on Massachusetts landlord/tenant law. She wrote her landlord a month before leaving, left the apartment in good condition and received her security deposit back (with interest) within ten days. That sure helped with moving costs and the information was free! Robin also learned that there are seventeen law libraries around the state that are free and can be used by anyone. So, if her local library didn't have the information, they could have directed her to a nearby law library.

Here are some of the books the public library offered:

Residential Landlord-Tenant Law: A Modern Massachusetts Guide by Phillip S. Lapatin & Herbert S. Lerman

Legal Tactics: Self Defense for Tenants in Massachusetts by National Lawyers Guild, Mass. Chapter.

Property Management Manual for Massachusetts Rental Owners by Housing Allowance Project Inc.

Visit your Public Library -- and learn your rights !

If you're finding the cost of modern life slightly unaffordable, you can't afford not to check out your public library!

Budget Stretcher # :

Lloyd Farmer discovered that "Where there's a will, there's a way (to save money)" -- thanks to his Public Library!

As Successor Trustee of his parents' Living Trust, Lloyd felt completely overwhelmed by the legal language and maze of requirements his duties demanded. But the library helped him "cut through the red tape" with information on wills, trusts, probate, executor's duties and powers of attorney.

Using several self-help volumes, Lloyd became informed and felt comfortable when he finally sought out legal advice. He knew that his time in the lawyer's office could be brief and to the point.

Visit your Public Library -- to be empowered and informed!

If you're finding the cost of modern life slightly unaffordable, you can't afford not to check out your public library!

DIRECTOR
ELLEN D. RAINVILLE

PROCLAMATION BY THE SELECTMEN/COUNCIL OF

_____

WHEREAS, An informed and thoughtful populace is integral to the success of a democratic nation, AND

WHEREAS, Public Libraries underscore those personal rights guaranteed by the Constitution and the Bill Rights, those being Freedom of Speech, Religious Belief and the Press (as evidenced in wide-ranging book collections), Freedom of Assembly (offered in the use of free meeting room space), and the Right to Privacy (upheld by confidential patron records and transactions), AND

WHEREAS, Public Libraries stand as an embodiment of the original ideals of the Constitution, offering the American populace free access to information and knowledge, cultural enrichment and recreation and personal growth and challenge in a democratic setting,

THEREFOR, WE THE SELECTMEN/COUNCIL OF THE TOWN/CITY OF _____ DO OFFICIALLY SALUTE THE _____ LIBRARY AND PROCLAIM RECOGNITION OF NATIONAL LIBRARY WEEK, APRIL 5 - 11, 1992.

SIGNED:

_____

_____

_____

_____

DATE: _____

50 MAIN STREET • WESTFORD, MASS. 01886

Library Awareness Campaign

Maine Library Association

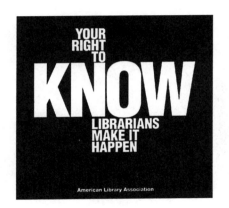

Maine Library Association
Library Awareness Campaign:
Marketing Your Right to Know
at the State and Local Levels

The LAC is a response by the MA to a recommendation from the 1991 Blaine House Conference, our pre-WHCLIST state conference, that "an effective marketing and public relations campaign at the federal, state, and local level must be mounted to promote services, increase awareness, and provide feedback to shape library and information services."

The MA Executive Council allocated $10,000 for a year-long effort to increase awareness not only of library resources but also of the problems confronting libraries. (As Prof. Herb White of Indiana University said at the 1990 MA conference, "Librarians are the only professionals who apologize to their users when budgets are cut." We want to change that!)

The sign-up for libraries was the first LAC activity. (Packet enclosed.) Results of the sign-up were released March 16, in time to promote the Call for America's Libraries. Newspaper coverage was fair, if not complete; there were 4 radio news stories and 1 news story.

The ALA "Right to Know" PSAs were duplicated for the cost of the blank tapes only by the media services dept. at the University of Southern Maine—a tag line crediting MA was added. The cassettes will be sent to librarians in the towns with the 29 major radio stations. (The MA PR committee will follow up with those librarians to be sure they did deliver the tapes.)

Coming up: the NBC affiliate in Portland will do public service spots featuring each of the elements of "Your Right to Know" ("how to participate in a democracy," "to have access to govt. information," etc.).

The "grocery bag" campaign is in the works. We've asked Hannaford Bros., owners of the largest supermarket chain in the region (Shop 'n Save), to print a "support your library" message on their bags with a trivia contest—answers available at the library, of course.

For more information, contact Nancy Blaine Hilyard, Auburn Public Library, 49 Spring St., Auburn, ME 04210; (207) 782-3191.

MLA
MAINE LIBRARY ASSOCIATION
1-800-452-8786
Local Government Center • RFD # 4, Box 35 • Augusta, Maine 04330 • (207) 623-8428

Dear Colleague:

We all know that libraries throughout Maine are facing shrinking budgets. To preserve the funding we need, we must recognize that the time has come for us to actively promote our libraries and the services we provide. This brings you the first activity of the MLA Public Relations Committee's year-long campaign to increase public awareness of and support for Maine libraries...and we hope you'll join us in our effort to make this campaign a success for all of us.

Enclosed is a sign-up statement to help demonstrate public support for libraries in Maine, and a poster asking people to take a moment to sign the statement. The goal of this statement is to give people an opportunity to express their backing for Maine libraries, and to generate attention to the fact that there *is* strong public support for libraries and the services they provide, so that spring budget deliberations this year can take that fact into account. The statement doesn't endorse any legislation or advocate any specific action; it simply demonstrates support and recognizes the need for adequate funding for libraries to be able to serve their users.

There are several ways you can use the statement and poster; choose whatever approach you feel most comfortable with:

- ■ You can display the poster and statement at your circulation desk or another high-traffic area of your library.

- ■ You can place copies of the statement and poster at other spots around town like the post office, town hall, community centers, etc. There are two copies of the poster enclosed; if you want to put statements out in more than two locations, simply make copies of the poster.

- ■ If you have Friends of the Library, ask them to take the statement around for signatures or put it out around town.

- ■ Meet with your board and ask them to put statements out where they feel they'll have the most impact.

Wherever you do put statements, make sure to make enough copies so that you won't run out of room for people to sign.

The Maine Library Awareness Campaign is a direct result of the survey commissioned by the Maine State Library as part of the Blaine House Conference on libraries. Among the survey findings were that a significant number of people in Maine do not know the variety of resources their libraries can provide, and that many people do not know how libraries are funded. Publicizing libraries was one of the recommendations approved by delegates to the Blaine House Conference.

The Maine Library Association has allocated $10,000 for such a project. The PR Committee has hired Marketing, Media & Wellman of Bangor to develop artwork, press releases, information kits, and other materials and events that will draw attention to the libraries in the state and their need for continuing support and increased funding. There will be a grassroots outreach by Committee members and others to enlist every librarian in taking part in this campaign, and this mailing is the first step in providing tools that you can use in your own community to help make the campaign work for you.

Please do what you can to get the statements out as soon as possible, because the cutoff date for collecting signatures is Friday, February 21. On the 21st, collect all the statements and count the total number of signatures on your statement sheets. (Each sheet has room for 25 signatures.) Then fill out the enclosed tally sheet and mail it to Marketing, Media & Wellman. Responses from all libraries will be compiled and released to newspapers, TV, and radio statewide just prior to the 1992 budget hearings and town meetings.

In the meantime, a separate response form is also enclosed so you can help us coordinate campign publicity efforts with your own activities. It lets us know how you plan to use the statements in your community, and lets you request copies of materials such as fact sheets being prepared for use with the media, town councils, and other key audiences. Please fill out the form and send it in the self-addressed envelope to Marketing, Media & Wellman. The more feedback we get, the better able we will be to ensure that statewide publicity releases go to the right places and people, and that you have the materials and support you need for your own publicity and community awareness activities.

If you have any questions or comments or would like to help with the library awareness campaign, please call Nann Hilyard at 1-782-3191. Use this statement during the budget preparation and hearing season! Take the statements to your city council or town meeting! Show the citizens of your town how many people use and appreciate the library! It's up to all of us to do it--because no one's going to do it for us.

Sincerely,
Nann B. Hilyard (MLA President)
&
Carolyn C. Hughes (PR Committee Chair)

The Maine Library Association: Working Together for Maine Libraries!

We're here for you. Be there for us.

PLEASE SIGN

These are tough times for libraries in Maine.
Show your support for this library,
and for libraries throughout
Maine, by taking a
moment to sign
this statement.

A Public Service Announcement by this Library
and The Maine Library Association.

A Statement in Support of Maine's Libraries.

**We the undersigned have affixed our names to this statement
to demonstrate our firm belief that:**

1. Maine's public, academic, school, and special libraries are a vital resource for the people of Maine.

2. Maine's libraries provide valuable services to students, businesses, families, and all the citizens of Maine, and access to those services is especially important in times of economic difficulty.

3. Maine's libraries deserve and should receive a level of funding sufficient to ensure that they can continue to provide services at current levels and continue to provide up-to-date resources to meet the changing needs of the people of Maine.

SIGNATURE	NAME (Please Print)	ADDRESS	DATE

MLA MAINE LIBRARY ASSOCIATION   1-800-452-8786

Local Government Center •   RFD # 4, Box 35 •   Augusta, Maine 04330 •   (207) 623-8428

Tally Sheet

**Please send by return mail to Marketing, Media & Wellman, One Cumberland Place,
Suite 102, Bangor, ME 04401, no later than Friday, February 21.**

Name of Library _____

Address _____

Director _____ **Phone** _____

**Other staff members or outside personnel involved in placing statements
and collecting signatures**

_____
_____
_____

Number of signatures collected _____

Other comments, etc. _____
_____
_____
_____
_____

MLA MAINE LIBRARY ASSOCIATION _____ 1-800-452-8786

Local Government Center • RFD # 4, Box 35 • Augusta, Maine 04330 • (207) 623-8428

Response Form

For coordinating campaign publicity and providing support materials.

Promote yourself, and let us help! Please fill out this form as soon as possible and return it to Marketing, Media & Wellman, One Cumberland Place, Suite 102, Bangor, ME 04401.

Once signatures on the sign-up statements are tallied from libraries around the state, press releases on the sign-up statement effort and the MLA Library Awareness Campaign will be issued to the major daily newspapers and television stations throughout Maine by Marketing, Media & Wellman. These releases will be accompanied by fact sheets on library usage and funding in Maine, library services, and other relevant issues of interest, so that editors and reporters will have background material with which to prepare stories.

We encourage you to work with your local media, too. If you have local weekly papers or other local media that you'd like to get the word out to about the sign-up statements and the Awareness Campaign, give them a call or send out your own news release about the sign-up statement, your services to the community, etc. Don't hesitate to promote your library, because people need to know what a bargain libraries are, and the extent of the services that are there for them to use--especially now, when there's closer scrutiny of budgets and operations.

If you do plan to send information to your local paper, it's a good idea to get in touch with the other libraries in your area so you can coordinate your efforts, and perhaps send one news release for all the libraries in the area rather than several different releases. If you'd like copies of the fact sheets, background papers, tips on working with the media, and other materials being prepared for the campaign to assist you, check off the box below and we'll send the materials to you.

Do you plan to use the signed statements to promote library awareness in your community, or do you plan other activities to promote your library and library awareness in general? Please describe briefly how you will be doing so. (For example, do you plan to send copies of statements to local media, town council, etc? Will you be meeting with your town council or doing some public outreach activities?) Please include a list of any print or broadcast media you will be contacting. _____

_____

_____

_____

_____

_____

Would you like to receive copies of the fact sheets and other materials being prepared for the Library Awareness Campaign? ☐ Yes ☐ No

Send materials to the attention of: Name _____

Address _____

If you have any specific information you would like us to include in our news releases to the major media in your area, please use the reverse side of this form to let us know.

NOTE: Please send copies of any press releases you send out and copies of any articles that appear in your local press, to Marketing, Media & Wellman so that we can compile a file of library media coverage from around the state. Thank you very much.

BACKGROUND PAPER

Crisis at Maine's Libraries:
A Look Around Maine

> Libraries across Maine are closing their doors, cutting their budgets, and eliminating services due to drastic cuts in state and local funding. Here's what's happening in just a few towns around the state.

- *Wilton: Wilton Free Public Library*—33% cut in books and magazine budget . . . no money for adult literacy or children's reading programs. . . maintenance budget cut 50%. . . equipment budget cut 33%. . . friends of the library group folded.

- *Winthrop: Charles M. Bailey Public Library*—All materials budgets frozen, unable to buy new books and magazines. . . sole source for new materials is gifts and donations.

- *Bath: Patten Free Public Library*—Circulation up 20% for January '92, but budget cut by $13,000.

- *Jonesport: Peabody Memorial Library*—Town appropriation cut by 28% since 1990. . . only able to stay open 12 hours a week.

- *Old Orchard Beach: Edith Belle Libby Memorial Library*—Book budget cut 78% since 1989-90, with more cuts expected. . . further cuts to force closing one day a week and cutting 6 hours pay per week for full time employees.

- *East Corinth: Central High School Library*—Budget for new materials cut 94%.

- *South Portland: South Portland Public Library*—Branch library closed after $50,000 budget cut, reopened for three days a week with volunteers and half-time staff after public outcry. . . branch book budget cut by 80%. . . main library hours reduced to only two nights a week.

- *Windham: Windham Public Library*—Book budget cut for 1992, further cuts expected.

- *Gray: Gray Public Library*—Budget freeze forces lapses in periodical supscriptions, prevents purchase of encyclopedia update. . . book budget cut back to 1988 level, library holds auction to raise money for books and magazines.

Maine Library Association
Local Government Center
RFD #4, Box 35
Augusta, Maine 04330
1-800-452-8786
(207) 623-8428

BACKGROUND PAPER

Libraries In America: Facts and Figures

Library Services

- *There are more libraries in America than there are McDonald's*--over 120,000. There are 92,538 elementary and high school libraries, 15,481 public libraries, 3,438 college and university libraries, and over 11,000 special libraries (corporate, medical, government, etc.).

- *79 million adults* a week use public libraries in America.
  49 million children a week use school libraries and media centers.
  14.2 million students, faculty (and the public) use college and university libraries each week.

- Public libraries in America circulate *over 1.3 billion items a year* for business and personal use, including books, videos, audiocassettes, computer software, and even toys and games.

- Libraries *save* business leaders, scientists and engineers an estimated *$19 billion a year* in information resources.

- *Two out of three* medium to large sized libraries offer space or staff for adult literacy training and/or testing.

- Research shows that spending for school library media services is the *single most important factor* related to student achievement.

- More children participate in library summer reading programs than in Little League baseball *(over 700,000 children every year)*.

Library Funding

- America's libraries serve up to *65% of the population* on a regular basis, yet they receive *only about 1%* of federal government spending.

- On a local level, library funding typically accounts for *only about 2%* of government spending. A 1991 survey of 60 libraries in Bergen County, New York showed that the average community spent just 1.4% of its tax bill on library funding.

- 25 years worth of federal library funding equals less than the cost of *one aircraft carrier,* or about $3.5 billion.

- Public libraries cost taxpayers *an average of $15.10 annually per capita*--less than dinner for two at a moderate restaurant.

Maine Library Association
Local Government Center
RFD #4, Box 35
Augusta, Maine 04330
1-800-452-8786
(207) 623-8428

BACKGROUND PAPER

What Do We Get From Libraries?

> These are just some of the things that Maine's libraries provide for all the people of Maine. All of these things and more are available to everyone, year-round, yet the total amount we spend on libraries in Maine is less than $15 per person per year. For all this, that's quite a bargain.

- Job listings and guides to employment openings around the country
- Career skills development materials
- Job searching how-to materials
- "Talking books" for the blind
- Literacy volunteer materials and adult literacy programs
- Information on state health programs
- Information referral for social services
- Business information: sales and marketing data, export/import assistance, listings of potential clients, and more
- On-line research services that let people search thousands of sources in seconds
- Free interlibrary loan service that lets people order materials from libraries around the world
- Current information on the status of pending congressional legislation
- FDA safety information on new products, and consumer buying guides
- How-to books and videos for the home and family
- Educational films
- Children's books
- Classic movies on video
- Research services for students, scholars, or anyone who wants to find information
- Large print books for people with difficulty reading small type
- State and federal government documents
- Local history and geneaological information
- Out-of-state newspapers
- Rare books and special materials
- The latest fiction and non-fiction bestsellers
- Community development materials
- Information on new drugs, on surgical procedures, on diseases, on supervising the care of a family member, and more
- Self-improvement books, books on coping with family problems, books on dealing with sexual abuse, drug and alcohol abuse, and more
- Tax forms, tax assistance guides, and other tax information
- Investment and personal finance materials to help people manage their money

Maine Library Association
Local Government Center
RFD #4, Box 35
Augusta, Maine 04330
1-800-452-8786
(207) 623-8428

BACKGROUND PAPER

What Is The Maine Library Association?

- The Maine Library Association is a non-profit association with 900 individual and institutional members.

- MLA represents all types of libraries... public, college and university, school, and corporate and other special libraries.

- MLA membership is open to anyone who is interested in libraries and librarianship in Maine.

- MLA is among the oldest state library associations in the United States. Since its founding in 1891, the Maine Library Association has worked to:

  - Develop and improve library service
  - Develop and maintain a statewide network to support and assist all libraries
  - Promote library interests in Maine
  - Promote public awareness of the services and programs available to Maine residents

What Does The MLA Do?

- MLA recommends minimum standards for Maine public libraries.

- MLA advocates intellectual freedom and provides support for those dealing with censorship challenges.

- MLA monitors state and federal legislation affecting libraries and encourages individuals to advocate goverment support for libraries.

- MLA offers continuing education opportunities to its members with courses, workshops, and annual conferences.

- MLA presents the Maine Student Book Award and the Lupine Award. In cooperation with the Maine Educational Media Association, MLA presents the annual SIRS Intellectual Freedom Award.

- MLA's student loan fund provides low-interest loans for graduate library education.

- MLA is a chapter of the New England Library Association and the American Library Association, linking the Maine library community with regional and national counterparts.

- MLA sections provide opportunities for librarians to exchange ideas and establish contacts in areas of particular interest, including Management and Administration; Children's and Young Adults' Services; Maine Online; Academic and Research Libraries; and other areas.

- The MLA publishes a quarterly journal, *The Maine Entry*, and a monthly newsletter, *Maine Memo*.

Maine Library Association
Local Government Center
RFD #4, Box 35
Augusta, Maine 04330
1-800-452-8786
(207) 623-8428

FACT SHEET

MA/NE'S LIBRARIES
MAINE LIBRARY AWARENESS CAMPAIGN

Libraries In Maine: Facts and Figures

- *There are over 860 libraries in Maine.* There are 238 public libraries, 500 school libraries, 22 college and university libraries, and an estimated 100 corporate and other special libraries.

- The average public library in Maine serves a population of about 3,500 people and has a circulation of over 27,950 items per year.

- *Maine has one of the highest per capita library circulation rates of any state in the U.S.* Nearly 6.5 books for each person in the state circulate from Maine's public libraries alone, compared to a national average of 5.6 books per person.

Library Usage in Maine vs. the National Average		
	Maine	U.S.
Circulation Per Capita	6.45	5.60
Interlibrary Loans Made (per 1,000 population)	33.87	19.07
Interlibrary Loans Received (per 1,000 population)	36.31	22.26

- In 1989, total expenditures by Maine's public libraries were $14.2 million. That was *less than one-half of one percent* of total state and local spending for that year.

- Most of Maine's public libraries have less than $1,000 a year to spend on books and other resources.

- *State per-capita aid and municipal appropriations, the two primary sources of funding for public libraries in Maine, are both being reduced.* State per capita aid has been eliminated altogether for FY 1992, and many municipalities are cutting library budgets to adjust to reduced income.

- *The majority of Maine's public libraries are open less than 20 hours a week* because they cannot afford to pay staff costs and energy bills to keep longer hours of service.

- The average public library budget in Maine in 1989 was $54,233, of which $9,073 was spent on the library's collection, $33,347 on staff salaries, and $11,813 on insurance, maintenance, supplies, and all other expenses. (*Most public libraries in Maine have much smaller budgets than these figures suggest, however. These averages reflect the larger budgets of major public libraries like Bangor, Portland, and Augusta.*)

A NOTE ON BOOK AND PERIODICAL PRICES:

Book and periodical prices are rising dramatically, magnifying the effect of library funding cuts. The average price of U.S. periodicals increased by 400% from 1977 to 1990, and the average price of a hardcover book more than doubled over the same period, from $19 to $41. Periodical prices are expected to rise by 11 to 13% in 1993. Book prices will also increase, although at a slightly slower rate.

Maine Library Association
Local Government Center
RFD #4, Box 35
Augusta, Maine 04330
1-800-452-8786
(207) 623-8428